Yes, Lord,
I Have Sinned,
But I Have Several
Excellent Excuses

Yes, Lord, I Have Sinned, But I Have Several Excellent Excuses

JAMES W. MOORE

Dimensions for Living
Nashville

YES, LORD, I HAVE SINNED,
BUT I HAVE SEVERAL EXCELLENT EXCUSES

Copyright © 1991 by Abingdon Press

Leader's Guide prepared by Shane Groth.

All rights reserved.

This book is printed on recycled, acid-free paper.

Library of Congress Cataloging-in-Publication Data

MOORE, JAMES W. (James Wendell), 1938–
    Yes, Lord, I have sinned, but I have several excellent excuses / James W.
    Moore.
    p. cm.
    ISBN 0-687-05383-8 (alk. paper)
    1. Sins—Sermons.   2. Forgiveness of sin—Sermons.   3. United Methodist
Church (U.S.)—Sermons.   4. Sermons, American.
    [1. Methodist Church—Sermons.]   I. Title.
    BV4625.M585   1991
    241'.3—dc20   90-40832
                                                                        CIP

Scripture at the beginning of chapters is from the New Revised Standard Version Bible, copyright © 1989, by the Division of Christian Education of the National Council of the Churches of Christ in the United States of America.

That noted NEB is from the New English Bible © The Delegates of the Oxford University Press and The Syndics of the Cambridge University Press 1961, 1970. Reprinted by permission.

Those noted KJV are from the King James Version of the Bible.

Many Scripture quotations are the author's own version.

03 04 — 20

MANUFACTURED IN THE UNITED STATES OF AMERICA

*For my family at home
and my special friends in the church
who have shared with me
the incredible good news
of God's amazing grace*

FOREWORD

As I read the original manuscript of *Yes, Lord, I Have Sinned, But I Have Several Excellent Excuses,* I was deeply impressed by the spiritual insights of my good friend Jim Moore. He deals with the sins that are most common in our churches and among Christians, and I felt pangs of guilt. However, he does not leave us on the floor of despair.

This book is not one that condemns, but one that brings hope and joy. It is about God's grace. These pages give us insight into our failures, but they also point out the paths to inner satisfaction and joy.

In the Bible we read about the Pharisees, and Dr. Moore has written a book that those Pharisees needed to read. They would have understood themselves better.

And we Christians today need to read this book, to better understand our silence, our halfheartedness, our rationalizations. We need the clear and loving answers Dr. Moore has given us—answers that inspire and lift us up, that challenge us and call us to deeper faith and commitment.

Jim Moore's personal friendship is a blessing to me. He is a kind and loving minister who understands people, and St. Luke's United Methodist Church, under his ministry, is truly an outstanding church.

As a preacher in the pulpit and over television and radio, Jim inspires great numbers of people and is heard with appreciation by various groups across America. I am glad he wrote *Yes, Lord, I Have Sinned, But I Have Several Excellent Excuses.*

Charles L. Allen

CONTENTS

Yes, Lord,
I Have Sinned,
But I Have Several
Excellent Excuses

1

Yes, Lord, I Have Sinned, But I Have Several Excellent Excuses!

Luke 14:15-24 One of the dinner guests, on hearing this, said to him, "Blessed is the one who will eat bread in the kingdom of God!" Then Jesus said to him, "Someone gave a great dinner and invited many. At the time for the dinner he sent his slave to say to those who had been invited, 'Come; for everything is ready now.' But they all alike began to make excuses. The first said to him, 'I have bought a piece of land, and I must go out and see it; please accept my regrets.' Another said, 'I have bought five yoke of oxen, and I am going to try them out; please accept my regrets.' Another said, 'I have just been married, and therefore I cannot come.' So the slave returned and reported this to his master. Then the owner of the house became angry and said to his slave, 'Go out at once into the streets and lanes of the town and bring in the poor, the crippled, the blind, and the lame.' And the slave said, 'Sir, what you ordered has been done, and there is still room.' Then the master said to the slave, 'Go out into the roads and lanes, and compel people to come in, so that my house may be filled. For I tell you, none of those who were invited will taste my dinner.' "

I don't know if you have noticed this, but we are living in very frank times! Nothing is kept under wraps anymore; we will admit to almost anything. We see people on national television laughing at their numerous marriage failures, admitting they are living together without being married, having children out of wedlock, openly telling of their use of drugs and alcohol. And are you ready for this?—the audience laughs and applauds! Our problem is not that we hesitate to *admit* anything; our problem is that we are

13

learning how to *justify* everything! We have excellent excuses for anything we want to do!

One of my favorite TV actors is Jack Klugman. I especially enjoyed his award-winning portrayal of the sloppy but lovable Oscar, on the long-running and successful comedy series "The Odd Couple." Later, Klugman became star of the dramatic series "Quincy," in which he played a medical examiner. In one of those episodes, there is a powerful dramatic scene in which Quincy confronts a doctor who had done a terrible thing and tried to cover it up. Quincy exposes the doctor's destructive deed, underscoring the fact that what the doctor did was not only illegal but also morally wrong.

The doctor is embarrassed; he winces and stammers a bit, then stands up from his desk and says, "I'm a busy man. I don't have time to talk about this now, so if you will please excuse me."

Quincy comes back with this penetrating response: "Doctor, I don't have the power to excuse you or what you have done. The question is, *Can you excuse yourself?*"

I don't know about that doctor, but what I have seen convinces me that we have become powerfully proficient at excusing ourselves. We have become amazingly eloquent at justifying our wrongdoings, excusing our worst sins.

At one point in Tolstoy's novel *War and Peace,* the main character Pierre is forced to face himself and make an honest analysis of his life. And he says it for all of us: *"Yes, Lord, I have sinned, but I have several excellent excuses!"*

Yes, we have several excellent excuses for just about everything we have done or might want to do. Whatever the situation, there is an ever-ready excuse available.

For One Thing, We Excuse Ourselves with Words.

TAKE THE MATTER OF MISSING CHURCH. Over the years, I have heard some great excuses for failure to make it to church. Some blame the weather, others blame company, still others blame their clothing. A man at one church fascinated me with his excuse. In the five years I was pastor there, he never once made it to church, but it seemed I was always running into him in crowded basketball arenas, in crowded theaters, or at crowded parties.

And he would always say, "Oh, Jim, I do wish I could come to church, but I can't stand to be in a crowd." I'm still trying to figure that one out!

However, my favorite reply was uttered by a woman: "I don't go to church, and this is my reason: If I go some of the time, it makes me want to go all the time. And since I can't go all the time, it makes me feel guilty when I miss some of the time. So I don't go any of the time, and this keeps me from feeling guilty about wanting to go all the time." Now, that's a *real* excuse, isn't it?

OR TAKE THE MATTER OF STEALING. I once heard this excuse from a young man who had been arrested for shoplifting: "I don't steal; I obtain. The store owners overcharge, so I am justified in obtaining some of the merchandise. It's all part of the game."

Or how about the young boy who took money out of his father's cash register, then excused himself by saying, "It wasn't my fault! He made me mad!"

THEN THERE IS PROFANITY. We try to justify it by calling it adult, honest, realistic speech. But what could be more childish, dishonest, or unreal?

WHAT ABOUT UNFAITHFULNESS? This is the most universally and amazingly justified sin in the world—all the way from the classic "My wife doesn't understand me" to "If you love somebody, why isn't it all right?" Why, it has even been called, of all things, the new morality. If we call it the *new* morality, we dupe ourselves, because it is the oldest *im*morality in the world.

AND TAKE THE MATTER OF GOSSIP. It is so dangerous, so cruel, so hurtful, so devastating, so sinful! And yet we indulge in it so frequently and excuse it so lightly. I once heard this excuse for gossip: "I won't tell anything about another person unless it is good—and boy, is this good!"

THEN THERE IS TEMPER. Have you ever heard someone say, "Oh, everybody knows I was born with a hot temper, but my temper is like a cyclone; it blows up quickly and blows away just as quickly." What people with a bad temper don't realize is that their temper, like a cyclone, also leaves behind immeasurable hurt, agony, heartache, and devastation.

WHAT ABOUT VENGEANCE? Again and again in the Gospels, Jesus warned us about the sin of the vengeful spirit, a spiritual cancer that will destroy our souls. "Don't give in to vengeance," he said, and yet we justify it and excuse it so neatly.

Remember how Archie Bunker put it: "What's wrong with revenge? It's the perfect way to get even." And I remember the story about two little boys who got into a fight on the schoolground. When the teacher went out to break it up, one little boy said, "He started it when he hit me back!"

Yes, we have sinned, but we have several excellent excuses! That's the first thing we do. We excuse ourselves with words—well-chosen words.

We Also Excuse Ourselves with Scapegoats.

Oh, how we like to put the blame on someone else! This ploy is as old as the Garden of Eden. Adam points at Eve, and Eve points at the serpent. The cry is, "It's not my fault," and the symbol is the pointing finger. Think of the way we use scapegoats to assuage our guilt.

And We Excuse Ourselves by Blaming Other People.

And we learn this tactic early. When our son Jeff was six years old, he went through a period of karate-chopping everything in sight. When he came into a room, he would karate-chop every piece of furniture!

One Saturday I was standing beside the sink when Jeff came karate-chopping his way into the kitchen. He karate-chopped the breakfast table, the chairs, and the refrigerator.

But when he karate-chopped the dishwasher, he accidentally hit the ON button. When the dishwasher started, Jeff stopped dead in his tracks.

He knew he had done something he shouldn't have, but quickly, he rose to the occasion.

He looked at me and said, "It's O.K., Dad, we'll tell Mom you did it!"

We Excuse Ourselves by Blaming Circumstances or Past Events.

Not long ago we took under our wing a fellow who seemed to have trouble getting and holding a job. He was going hungry, and we were concerned about him, so we found him a job. He worked one day and quit. We found him another job, and again he worked one day and quit. When we got him the third job, he worked two days and quit.

We finally said to him, "We owe you an apology. We're getting you the wrong kind of job. What seems to be the problem?"

He said, "It's all because of the food poisoning."

"Oh, we're sorry," we said. "We didn't know. When did you have food poisoning?"

He answered, "During the spring of 1947." We excuse ourselves by blaming past events.

Finally, We Excuse Ourselves by Blaming Evil Spirits.

Flip Wilson's phrase, "The devil made me do it," can cover a multitude of sins. The idea here is that our behavior can be controlled by demons.

"I'm not responsible," we say. "The devil got into me." That's a good excuse!

I saw a cartoon about this notion recently. A woman had bought a very expensive new dress, and her husband asked why she had been so extravagant.

She replied, "The devil made me do it."

"Well," the husband asked, "why didn't you say 'Get thee behind me, Satan!' ?"

"I did," explained the wife. "But he said the dress looked as good in the back as it did in front, so I bought it."

This is a light treatment of a very serious subject. Ever since the book and movie *The Exorcist* came out, I have been asked if I believe we are the helpless victims of evil spirits. My answer to that is an emphatic *No!* I do not believe our God would subject us to anything that would leave us powerless or cut us off from the abundant life Jesus came to share with us. We have free will. We have choice . . . and the truth is that we sometimes choose poorly. Then we try to cover up with scapegoats. Yes, we have sinned, but we have several excellent excuses . . . and scapegoats.

What Does the Christian Faith Say About Excuses?

FIRST, GOD SEES THROUGH OUR EXCUSES. Like a parent who knows all the children well, God knows us. God can't be conned! God knows us better than we know ourselves. God sees through us and our excuses. Our excuses seem so frail and feeble under the light of God.

That is what the strange little parable in Luke 14 is about. A man is giving a great banquet. The invitation goes out: Come! All is ready! Then there is that haunting line, "But they all alike began to make excuses."

One man is a farmer: "I have bought a field; I have business responsibilities. I pray you, have me excused." The second is a cattleman: "I've just bought five yoke of oxen. I must go examine them. I pray you, have me excused." The third man says: "I've married a wife and therefore I cannot come." (Note the play on male humor here. The farmer and the cattleman politely ask to be excused, but the married man says, "You know I can't come—I'm married.") As someone once put it, "He took it like a man—he blamed it on his wife!" So the man had the party without them.

The story has some strange elements, but one central truth here needs to be underscored: We can make excuses for almost anything we want to do or don't want to do, but God sees through them—and our excuses may be the very things that are keeping us out of God's party . . . out of God's kingdom and out of God's presence.

SECOND, GOD IS MORE INTERESTED IN FORGIVING OUR SINS THAN IN HEARING OUR EXCUSES. We don't need a scapegoat; we have a Savior. Christ came to show us that forgiveness is at hand. We see it powerfully in the parable of the prodigal son in Luke 15.

The prodigal, as he comes home penitent, is rehearsing his confession: "Father, I have sinned against heaven and against you; I'm no longer worthy to be called your son; treat me as one of your hired servants." I can see him walking down the road, repeating that over and over, getting the inflection and the emphasis just right. But notice that when he reaches home, the father runs to meet him!

A careful reading reveals something very significant here. When the son begins to blurt out his confession, the father interrupts. He doesn't want to hear it. He wants to get on with the party, the celebration. Forgiveness was there, available all along. The prodigal needed only to come back and accept it. No more talk needed, no excuses necessary.

"Bring the best robe and put it on him. Put a ring on his hand and shoes on his feet. . . . Let's have a feast, for this my son was dead and he is alive again; he was lost but now is found."

Here's the point—we're not justified by our eloquent excuses but by the grace of a loving, caring, forgiving God!

THIRD, WHAT GOD WANTS FROM US IS NOT EXCUSES, BUT PENITENCE. What is said with the lips is not nearly as important as what happens in the heart. We see this dramatically in Luke 18, Jesus' parable of the Pharisee and the publican who go up to the Temple to pray.

The Pharisee tries to "excuse" himself. He tries to cover his guilt with words: "Lord, I do this, I do that, I do the other." And then he tries scapegoats: "And I thank you, Lord, that I'm not like these other men, especially like this publican." On and on he goes—words, excuses, scapegoats, cover-ups.

But there is the publican with his prayer of penitence. He bows his head reverently, beats upon his chest and cries, "God, be merciful to me, a sinner." As the parable closes, it is clear that the penitent publican was justified, rather than the excuse-making Pharisee.

Have you heard about the minister who dreamed that he had died and was trying to get into heaven? When he approached the gates, Saint Peter told him he needed 100 points to get in.

Proudly the minister said, "Well, I was a minister for 43 years."

"That's fine," said Peter. "That's worth one point."

"One point? Is that all?" cried the minister. "Just one point for 43 years of service?"

"Yes, that's correct," answered Peter.

"Well, I visited shut-ins."

"One point."

"I worked with young people."

"One point."

"I developed a number of fine Scout programs."

"One more point. That makes four points. You need 96 more."

"Oh, no!" said the minister, in a panic. "I feel so helpless, so inadequate. Except for the grace of God, I don't have a chance!"

Saint Peter smiled and said, *"Grace of God—96 points! Come on in!"*

That minister's dream is rooted in a strong theological reality—our hope is the grace of God.

What God wants is not excuses, but penitence and commitment. Yes, we have sinned, and we have several excellent excuses, but God sees through them. And he's much more interested in forgiveness, penitence, and commitment, anyway.

The Sin of Just Talking
a Good Game

Matthew 23:23-28 "Woe to you, scribes and Pharisees, hypocrites! For you tithe mint, dill, and cummin, and have neglected the weightier matters of the law: justice and mercy and faith. It is these you ought to have practiced without neglecting the others. You blind guides! You strain out a gnat but swallow a camel!

"Woe to you, scribes and Pharisees, hypocrites! For you clean the outside of the cup and of the plate, but inside they are full of greed and self-indulgence. You blind Pharisee! First clean the inside of the cup, so that the outside also may become clean.

"Woe to you, scribes and Pharisees, hypocrites! For you are like whitewashed tombs, which on the outside look beautiful, but inside they are full of the bones of the dead and of all kinds of filth. So you also on the outside look righteous to others, but inside you are full of hypocrisy and lawlessness."

Have you ever heard someone make a point by somehow coming up with just the right words? It's a good feeling when you are able to find the perfect words at just the right moment. I have seen this happen many times.

It took place once on a family vacation. We were driving down an interstate highway in Florida. The children were pretty young then—Jodi was eight, and Jeff was six. Out of the blue, Jodi announced that she was going to be a jet pilot when she grew up.

Younger brother Jeff, disturbed by the prospect of that, retorted, "Jodi, there is no way you are going to be a jet pilot!"

"Why not?" she asked.

"Because!" Jeff went on. "Because you are a girl, and all jet pilots are men. You can't be a jet pilot because you are a girl!"

Then came the response, perfectly given as only a big sister could express it: "And you, little brother," she said, "are a *male chauvinist piglet!*" Just the right words for the situation!

Now, all of us have known that experience of finding the perfect words for the occasion, the right words to make our point, the ideal words for the situation. Unfortunately, however, the reverse is also true. Sadly, all of us also have known those awful, agonizing moments when we were at a complete loss for words, when we were reduced to an embarrassing, shameful silence.

This has happened to me many times. I once complimented a woman on her beautiful maternity dress . . . to which she replied acidly, "For your information, this is *not* a maternity dress!" Now, what can you say to that? *I* didn't know what to say. I couldn't even stammer out an apology. I was reduced to an embarrassed silence.

Sometimes we *are* at a complete loss for words, but the truth is that most of the time we do pretty well with words; we are fairly eloquent. We talk a pretty good game, but our real problem is with actions, with follow-through. We talk too much and do too little! We verbalize so well and actualize so poorly! We speak so eloquently and perform so inadequately! We spout high-sounding words, then put off acting until tomorrow! But we *must* see that talking a good game is not enough! Only when our words are translated into action are they authenticated.

And nowhere is this more true than with matters of faith. It's not enough to just hear it preached from our pulpits. It's not enough to just sing it in our hymns. It's not enough to just talk about it in our Sunday school classes. Faith is a life-style—a way of living! This is what Paul meant when he wrote these words: "Let your manner of life be worthy of the gospel of Christ"—that is, let your conduct, your behavior, your actions, your tone of voice, *your everyday life,* be worthy of Christ.

Paul is right on the mark here, because Christianity is not merely a set of intellectual ideas, a collection of theological beliefs, a series of philosophical arguments. It is a *way of life,* a way of acting and responding, a way of relating to God and to people. *It's a life-style—a life-style that works!* Christianity is not just a way of believing; it is also a way of behaving. Our faith is not just something we proclaim and celebrate in the sanctuary; it is something we live out and demonstrate and share with others at home, in the office, on the street, on the tennis court, even on a date.

I ran across a true story about something that happened in Africa some years ago that makes the point well. Some missionaries were going into a remote corner of Africa to work with a primitive tribe. The missionaries didn't know how they would be received, so they decided to give the tribe a gift as a sign of goodwill. They flew over the area and dropped a bright, shiny new plow by parachute. A few days later, when the missionaries arrived, they found something they hadn't counted on. The natives had never seen a plow before and didn't know how to use this strange-looking instrument which had dropped mysteriously from the skies. And so, not knowing what else to do with it, they had put the plow on a pedestal and were worshiping it!

That plow, of course, was designed to be used, not revered. It was designed to strike deep into the African soil and produce food for their tables. It was designed to work for the people, to help the people, to nourish the people, make them healthier, make their quality of life better. But the members of that primitive tribe didn't know that, so the plow became an ornament, rather than a tool!

This is what we are always tempted to do with our faith: make it an ornament rather than a tool; think of it as an object of veneration, rather than a means to personal and social transformation; see it as a lovely set of ideals to be laid neatly upon a pedestal, rather than as a powerful force designed to revolutionize our manner of life—and indeed the whole fabric of society.

This was what so upset the eighth-century prophets. This is why Amos, Micah, Hosea, and Isaiah became so angry with the people of their time. This is why those great prophets cried out so dramatically. They felt, and rightly so, that unless our religion changes our life, it is a farce; unless our faith touches our moral behavior, it is just hypocritical play-acting! Liturgies, ceremonies, and holy feasts were good if they helped produce righteous lives; otherwise, they were a stench in the nostrils of God! Strong language, but that's what the prophets said. They spoke out for God: "I hate your feasts, I despise your ceremonies. I want love and truth and kindness and righteousness—not sacrifices and burnt offerings!"

The point is clear: Talking a good game is not enough. *Unless creeds are translated into deeds,* they become dull, insipid, dead, worthless. If our faith is not lived out, if we don't practice what we preach, if our Christian profession doesn't burst forth into Christian expression, then it is but "sound and fury" that signifies nothing!

Only When Our Creeds Become Deeds
Do They Become Compelling.

Only when our words and our beliefs are translated into actions do they really take hold of our lives. Some years ago, John Mott decided to try to really discover the meaning and power of prayer. He attended lectures on prayer. He listened to sermons on prayer. He researched the biblical references to prayer. He read everything he could get his hands on about prayer, but he came up empty. Then he discovered the answer—he started to pray! He made prayer

an active part of his life. He said that he had read
seventy-two books on prayer, but it wasn't until he started to
pray that prayer became a real compelling force in his life!

That's the way it works. We can recite our creeds, and we
should. We can study our Scriptures, and we should. We can
research our doctrines, and we should. But only when our
faith is translated into action, only when our beliefs take
root in our daily living—only then is our religion worth its
salt, only then is our Christianity compelling.

Only When Our Creeds Become Deeds
Do They Become Contagious.

Doctrines, creeds, ideas, beliefs—no matter how true, no
matter how eloquent, no matter how perfectly phrased—
carry very little conviction in themselves. It is when they
walk before us in flesh and blood that they become
contagious.

That's how it is with the Christian faith. The truths of our
religion are most impressive, most inspiring, most influen-
tial when they are wrapped up in living persons. God knows
that. That's why he sent Jesus—so we could see his *truth*
wrapped up in a person. The most effective argument for
Christianity is a real Christian. The supreme argument for
our holy faith is a holy life. The truth is that the people out
there on the street are not that interested in our theologies,
or our liturgies, or our vestments. The people out there are
pragmatists. They want to know, "Does this thing work?"
They are tremendously interested in that.

In *Twelve Tests of Character*, Harry Emerson Fosdick
gave an illustration that makes this point dramatically. He
told that during the course of the atrocities that occurred in
Armenia during the early part of this century, a Turkish
soldier had chased a young woman and her brother down the
street into a dead-end alley. Although the soldier killed the
brother, the young woman escaped. Later, however, she

was captured and, since she was a nurse, was put to work in a military hospital.

Then one day the soldier who had murdered her brother was brought into the hospital and placed in her ward! Terror flashed over his face as their eyes met and they recognized each other.

The soldier was critically wounded, and the nurse knew that the slightest inattention would cause his death. She struggled within. One part of her cried out for vengeance—Here is your chance! No one will ever know. But the spirit of Christ won out. She conscientiously and tenderly nursed him back to health, and each evening she prayed for him.

Later, he asked, "Why? You recognized me. Why did you care for me so faithfully?"

She replied, "Because I serve him who said, 'Love your enemies and do them good.' That is my faith."

After a quiet moment, the Turkish soldier said, "Tell me more of your religion. Tell me more of your Lord. I would give anything to have a faith like yours!"

Only when our creeds become deeds do they really become compelling and contagious!

***Only When Our Creeds Become Deeds
Do They Become Convincing.***

A friend told a wonderful story that speaks to this. Several years ago, a teacher assigned to tutor children in a large city hospital was asked to help a young boy who had been seriously burned in an accident. The boy's regular teacher told the tutor that the class was studying irregular verbs and dangling participles; she was concerned that without help during his extended hospital stay, the boy might fall too far behind.

When the visiting teacher went to see the youngster, she was horrified to discover that he was in the critical care unit. He had been burned so badly all over his body that he could barely talk. She tried her best to work with him on irregular verbs and dangling participles, but when she left, she honestly didn't know whether she had helped him.

However, when the tutor returned the next day, the head nurse was all smiles: "You worked a miracle yesterday! We have been so worried about that boy. He had been so depressed and unresponsive. He had given up. He was just lying there, waiting to die. But after you came, his attitude changed. He is talking. He is working with us. He is fighting back, and he's beginning to respond to treatment. And now we believe he's going to make it!" The teacher was pleased, but dumbfounded. She had no idea what she had done to cause such a change.

After the boy was released from the hospital, he explained why the teacher's visit had made such a difference. A simple realization had come to him that night after the teacher left.

He said, "They told me I would live, but I didn't believe them. I thought they were just saying that. But when that teacher came, it made all the difference. I realized they wouldn't send a teacher to work with a dying boy on irregular verbs and dangling participles!"

They had told him he would live, but he wasn't convinced. The action of that teacher, coming to help him with his homework, made all the difference! Actions speak louder than words! Actions are more compelling, more contagious, and more convincing. An unknown poet expressed it like this:

We are writing a Gospel a chapter each day
By deeds that we do and words that we say;
People read what we write, whether faithless or true . . .
So *what is the gospel according to you?*

3

The Sins That Reduce Us
to Shameful Silence

Mark 9:33-37 Then they came to Capernaum; and when he was in the house he asked them, "What were you arguing about on the way?" But they were silent, for on the way they had argued with one another who was the greatest. He sat down, called the twelve, and said to them, "Whoever wants to be first must be last of all and servant of all." Then he took a little child and put it among them; and taking it in his arms, he said to them, "Whoever welcomes one such child in my name welcomes me, and whoever welcomes me welcomes not me but the one who sent me."

Let me begin with a question: Have you ever been reduced to an embarrassed silence—the kind of silence that comes from a sense of shame, from doing wrong and being found out, from suddenly realizing that you have short-cut your best self?

There is a haunting example of this kind of silence in Mark's Gospel. Jesus is heading toward Jerusalem and the cross when his disciples begin to bicker and quarrel about which of them should be greatest in the Kingdom. Can you picture this in your mind? To me, there is something painfully heartbreaking in this scene. On the one hand is Jesus, moving steadfastly toward the cross, his face set toward Jerusalem—resolved, committed—surely thinking deep thoughts about the confrontation certain to come in the Holy City, determined to stand tall and firm; to do God's will; to strike a blow for justice; to face it all head-on, come what may.

On the other hand, here are the disciples walking along behind him, completely misunderstanding the Kingdom, thinking of it in simplistic, selfish, materialistic terms, and of themselves as the prestigious chiefs of state. Bickering and quarreling over who should have the most important positions, they are not aware that Jesus is hearing them. But he is.

He stops, turns, and asks, "By the way, what were you discussing?" Now with that question, they know that he knows, "but they were silent." Think about that heavy phrase: "But they were silent." They were reduced to the silence of shame, an embarrassed silence, so ashamed of their pettiness that they were speechless.

Isn't it fascinating the way things take their proper place and acquire their true character when they are set before the eyes of Christ, played back in the presence of Christ? As long as they thought Jesus was not hearing them, the argument about who should be greatest seemed fair enough, but when it was necessary to state that argument in Jesus' presence, it was exposed in all its unworthiness!

This raises some penetrating questions, doesn't it? If Christ knew what we were doing, would we be embarrassed? If Christ heard what we were saying, would we be ashamed? If Christ knew what we were thinking and feeling, would we be red-faced and speechless? Be candid with yourself for a moment. Have you ever been reduced to an embarrassed, shameful silence? I guess if the truth were known, we all have.

- I'm thinking of a group of people engaged in a rather cruel gossip session, talking harshly about another person, when suddenly that person walks unannounced into the room, and there is an awkward, embarrassed silence.
- I'm thinking of some teenagers thumbing through some

questionable literature, when suddenly Mother appears at the door, and there is an awkward, embarrassed silence.

- I'm thinking of a group of men exchanging shady stories, when suddenly right in the middle of one of the stories—perhaps at the most profane moment—someone they respect and admire greatly walks up unexpectedly; again, an awkward, shameful silence.
- I'm thinking of some office workers who are loafing on the job, wasting valuable time, when suddenly the boss walks in. And quietly, quickly, abashedly, they slip back to their workplaces.

Do any of these situations sound at all familiar? Being caught like this can be a very agonizing experience. How well we know!

When I was in the fourth grade, I had a red-faced moment like that, and it is still vivid in my memory. It happened in the school library. As fourth-graders, we were being allowed more freedom in the library, and on this particular day as I was browsing around, my eyes fell on a strange book title. I couldn't believe it—a book with a title containing an unmentionable four-letter word in the school library! This was the late 1940s, and to see a four-letter word in print back then was shocking indeed! As I pulled the book off the shelf and examined it, I understood what had happened. The real title of the book was *Hello, the Boat!* but somehow over the years, the last letter—the *o*—in the word *Hello* had been rubbed out. As a nine-year-old in the fourth grade, I thought this was hilarious—a four-letter word in the school library!

Snickering, I began to motion for my friends and classmates to share in this terrific scoop. One by one, they came and I proudly pointed out my discovery.

We were giggling and snickering when suddenly I felt a hand on my shoulder and heard a question: "What have you boys found over here that is so interesting?" We turned and looked up into the face of the librarian, and we were reduced to an embarrassed silence—especially me, because I had started it, I was holding the book. And not only was she the librarian at school, she was also my Sunday school teacher!

I can remember the agony of that moment as if it were yesterday—my flushed face, my emotional pain, my embarrassment, the feeling that she was disappointed in me. I was totally speechless. I had no defense, no excuse, no explanation. I had been found out, and I was experiencing the agony of being reduced to silence—the silence of shame.

Take that feeling to a deeper level, and you can understand what happened to the disciples that day as they traveled with Jesus on the road to Jerusalem. What were the disciples doing, saying, feeling, that later came back to haunt them? What attitudes were they expressing, that later, in the presence of Christ, seemed so petty and unworthy? What was it that reduced them to a shameful silence? Three things—ruthless ambition, bitter jealousy, bickering hostility. When we look at those three things, we may find ourselves somewhere between the lines.

First, They Were Silenced by Their Ruthless Ambition.

Ambition, in and of itself, is a good thing, a natural, normal part of our makeup. We all want to be important. We want recognition. We want to achieve distinction. So ambition is basically a good quality. It becomes bad only when distorted or misused. When it becomes selfish and ruthless, then it is a monstrous, destructive tyrant.

That's what was brewing in their group that day. Each disciple was saying, in his own way, "I will get ahead, no matter who I have to step on or push aside. If I need to elbow other people out of the way, then so be it." This is the picture of selfish, ruthless ambition. Not a very pretty picture, is it?

In another place in Mark's Gospel, James and John have the audacity to ask Jesus for the two best positions in his kingdom. They were trying to slip in ahead of the other disciples—especially Simon Peter. It's interesting to note that when Matthew told the same story later, he tried to soften it by saying that the mother of James and John made the request! This is an obvious attempt to clean up the act a bit, to cover for James and John and their selfish ambition. You see, it's much more understandable for a mother to make this kind of request. But it can't really be covered up. In the economy of God, the truth will come out, and ruthless ambition, when it is uncovered and exposed, will reduce us to shameful silence.

"Ruthless" ambition—where did that word *ruthless* come from? I'm not sure, but here is an intriguing thought: What if it came from the story of Ruth in the Old Testament? Ruth is the symbol of love and loyalty, thoughtfulness and faithfulness. She puts others before herself and expresses tender concern for Naomi, her mother-in-law. It was Ruth who said, "Whither thou goest, I will go; and where thou lodgest, I will lodge: thy people shall be my people, and thy God my God" (Ruth 1:16 KJV). In Ruth, we see the epitome of loyalty, the symbol of unselfish love.

To be "ruth-less" then, must be the opposite—that is, to be without the spirit of Ruth. And that was the problem with the disciples that day as they quarreled over position. They had forgotten their holy writings. They had forgotten the spirit of Ruth. Their ambition was ruthless. That was their problem, and maybe it is our problem, too.

Someone once described the danger of this kind of ambition. That story is about a man who was told that he could claim all the land he could walk around in one day, from sunrise to sunset. The man jumped at the opportunity. He began leisurely, glad for his strong legs, but as he walked, the lure for more and more stirred within him. If he walked faster, he could circle more land. The farther he went, the more land he wanted, and soon he began to run. He burned with fever. He gasped for breath. But he could not stop, he could not rest. One word—*more*—reverberated in his brain. At last the sun began to sink and his legs began to fail. He threw off his shirt, then his boots. His heart was pounding now like a drum. Forcing his body to the utmost, just as the sun fell beyond the horizon, he lunged forward and touched the goal with his fingertips. He had made it! But he had really failed, for he dropped there, dead! They took a shovel and gave him his land—a strip of soil, six by two, for his grave!

The point is clear—this kind of ambition can destroy us! But notice in Mark's story that Jesus does not abolish ambition—he redeems it! He tells the disciples to be ambitious, but for *others!* Be ambitious to be a servant!

Recently I ran across a delightful story about a little boy who was in church one Sunday morning with his grandmother. All went well until offering time. Then the grandmother began to search frantically through her purse for her offering envelope, but she couldn't find it. She had left her gift at home. Embarrassed, she kept looking through her purse for something to put in the collection plate.

Sensing her dilemma, the little boy rose to the occasion: "Here, Gramma, you take my quarter and put it in, and I'll hide under the seat!"

Now, that's a light treatment of a very significant spirit—the spirit of being ambitious to help others! That's what Jesus wanted. And the disciples knew it. They knew that selfishness wouldn't really fit into his kingdom, and when their selfishness was exposed, they were reduced to silence.

They Were Silenced by Their Jealousy.

Ruthless ambition and jealousy—I guess those two things go hand in hand, don't they? Author J. Wallace Hamilton, in *Ride the Wild Horses,* talks about how much we like to be praised:

> We like it even when we know we don't deserve it. We like it when we don't believe it, and as someone has said, we dislike it only when we hear it bestowed too much on others. Bishop Berry used to say that if a man can enjoy hearing his predecessor praised or his competitor complimented, he is qualified as an authority on the doctrine of entire sanctification. (p. 28)

Jealousy—how dangerous it is! It will not fit in the Kingdom.

Finally, They Were Reduced to Silence by Their Hostility.

They were quarreling, bickering, arguing. Even as Jesus, the Master of love, moves toward the cross, his closest followers, his most intimate friends, are seething with hostility. There is a certain pathos about this. They have heard him preach and teach love; they have sensed his spirit of humility and compassion; they have seen his acts of loving kindness. And yet here they seem to have missed his main point.

Jesus had to go to the cross to get their attention! There on the cross, he showed them and he showed us, that love (not hostility), love (not jealousy), love (not selfish ambition)— *love* is life as God meant it to be!

This quarreling of the disciples bothered Jesus. Hostile bickering has no place in his kingdom. When are we going to learn that?

So he stopped and dealt with their bickering quite seriously. Notice the words in Mark 9: "He sat down [and] called the twelve." In Jesus' time, teachers would walk about teaching, instructing, pointing out truths along the way; but when they wanted to say something authoritative, something of supreme importance, they sat down! Remember the Sermon on the Mount. Jesus went up on the mountain and *sat down* to preach, and here Jesus again sits down and teaches them authoritatively, teaches them to be servants, to be humble, to be trusting, to be loving.

Jesus was disturbed by their ambition, their jealousy, their hostility—and for good reason. Maybe it's because he knew that those same things awaited him in Jerusalem. A scant few days later, those same destructive attitudes—selfish ambition, jealousy, hostility—nailed Jesus to a cross! Those attitudes put him there. And it's still happening today! Every time we demonstrate those attitudes, we are crucifying God's Truth, and somewhere along the way we will answer for it.

But the good news is that, ultimately, in God's own time, his truth and his love will win the day, and then ruthless ambition, bitter jealousy, bickering hostility will be reduced forever to shameful silence!

4

The Sin of Halfheartedness

Matthew 5:38-45 "You have heard that it was said, 'An eye for an eye and a tooth for a tooth.' But I say to you, Do not resist an evildoer. But if anyone strikes you on the right cheek, turn the other also; and if anyone wants to sue you and take your coat, give your cloak as well; and if anyone forces you to go one mile, go also the second mile. Give to everyone who begs from you, and do not refuse anyone who wants to borrow from you.

"You have heard that it was said, 'You shall love your neighbor and hate your enemy.' But I say to you, Love your enemies and pray for those who persecute you, so that you may be children of your Father in heaven; for he makes his sun rise on the evil and on the good, and sends rain on the righteous and on the unrighteous."

A few years ago, I was on the campus of a small college during its Religious Emphasis Week. The theme of the week was "The Hard Sayings of Jesus"—that is, the difficult teachings of Jesus.

One evening I was leading a discussion on some of these difficult teachings: "Turn the other cheek"; "Love your enemies"; "Go the second mile"; "Pray for those who persecute you."

One young man said, "The teachings of Jesus are difficult for me because I'm not sure I understand them."

Another student said, "I see it just the other way around. They are difficult for me because I think I *do* understand them . . . but I'm not so sure I want to do them."

When you study the Gospels closely, you come face to face with the frustrating fact that Jesus did indeed say some perplexing things. These "difficult" sayings have puzzled many devout Bible readers over the years. Even during his ministry, Jesus often was misunderstood by his hearers— even by his own disciples. A vivid example occurs in John 6:60. Some of the disciples, after hearing Jesus speak, exclaim, "This is a hard saying; who can listen to it?"

The New English Bible makes it even more dramatic by translating it this way: "This is more than we can stomach! Why listen to such talk?" Then a few verses later, we find this haunting sentence: "From that time on, many of his disciples withdrew and no longer went about with him" (6:66).

This reveals something very interesting—that the difficulty here is not just in understanding what Jesus meant, but in a real sense, we could say that when we understand these difficult sayings, our difficulty has just begun! It has just begun because now we run head on into the startling challenges of living the Christian faith.

As Jesus saw it, being a Christian disciple meant living in a special spirit—a sacrificial, self-giving spirit, which unfortunately, many of us are afraid to try! You may call it magnanimity, or generosity, or bigness, or graciousness, or selflessness, or unconditional love. But whatever label you put on it, Jesus is saying, "Live in this spirit!" And that's where the real difficulty begins. He is saying:

- Respond to harshness with kindness.
- Respond to cruelty with tenderness.
- Respond to hurt with forgiveness.
- Respond to adversity with perseverance.
- Respond to hate with love.

Can Jesus really mean this? The world scoffs and says with the disciples, "Wait a minute, now. This is more than we can stomach. How can we listen to this? There must be some

mistake here. Life doesn't work that way!" But don't you
see? Jesus is saying that this is precisely the way life *will*
work, if only we could be bold enough to believe it and try it.

- A soft answer does indeed turn away wrath.
  (If you don't believe that, try it!)
- Forgiveness is indeed better than vengeance, every
  time.
- Love is indeed the most powerful thing in the world.

The only way you and I can be authentic disciples of Christ
is to believe that, stake our lives on it, and give our lives to it.
To live in this gracious spirit is the calling of every Christian.
It is the main message of the Sermon on the Mount (Matt. 5,
6, 7). Again and again and again he hammers it home to us.
Live in this spirit, live in this unselfish, gracious, forgiving
spirit!

The real difficulty here is not so much in understanding
what Jesus meant. "Love your enemies. Pray for those who
persecute you." We know what that means, but we are not
so sure we want to do it. The real difficulty comes when we
realize that Jesus meant what he said. He meant it so much
that he gave his life for it, lost his life doing it. He meant it so
much that he saw these sacrificial qualities as the most
authentic marks of Christian discipleship. The real difficulty
here is believing what Jesus said enough to try doing it.

Well, what do you think? Do you believe what Jesus
taught enough to try it? Do his teachings still work? Do they
fit today's world? Jesus' teachings are beautiful, even
provocative, but are they practical in a world like ours? Our
world is hard-nosed and cynical, calloused, power hungry,
sometimes even violent. "Go the second mile." "Lay down
the sword." "Be meek." "Love your enemies." What
possible relevance do such soft-sounding attitudes have for
this hard, tough world? There has been a lot of discussion
about this over the years. Brilliant scholars have debated it.

- Some scholars say, "This may work in personal life, but certainly not in international affairs."
- Some say, "It's an interim ethic. Jesus felt the end of the world was coming soon, and he was giving us an interim ethic, a way to live in those final days before the end of time."
- Others say, "He meant what he said, just as he said it, and the problem is that we don't have the courage to try it!"

Well, what do you think? Do you believe he meant it? Are you willing to try it?

Now, let's look at one of the hardest sayings to swallow. Jesus told us to turn the other cheek: "You have heard that it was said, 'An eye for an eye and a tooth for a tooth.' But I say to you, do not resist an evildoer. But if anyone strikes you on the right cheek, turn the other also."

Turn the other cheek—what in the world is Jesus talking about here? What can this mean? Let me suggest a few ideas.

When Jesus tells us to turn the other cheek, he means . . .

Don't Retaliate.

He means that we should not return hurt for hurt. Two wrongs don't make a right. Don't feel that you must "get even." Jesus lived out this philosophy of bigness of spirit. These are not just idle idealistic words; rather, they represent the life-style of the Christian, the spirit of magnanimity and grace. Jesus suffered many hurts—blows and insults of all kinds—but he never retaliated. He was too big for that.

There's an old story about two farmers who lived side by side. One day the fence between the two farms was pushed down, and the livestock of one farmer trampled the garden of the other farmer. The farmer whose garden was damaged was so irate that he rounded up the animals and refused to return them until their owner had paid in full for the damages. The farmer whose livestock had caused the problem was genuinely sorry. He apologized, paid the damages, took his cows home, and repaired the fence.

A few days later, ironically, the opposite thing happened! The other man's livestock pushed the fence down and got into the other garden. But this farmer, who had a golden opportunity to retaliate, chose to come at the problem in a different way. He rounded up the cows and returned them to their owner.

The owner, red-faced and embarrassed, reached for his checkbook: "I suppose you have the damages figured, so let me pay you and get it over with. How much do I owe you?"

"Nothing, nothing at all, not a penny," said the good farmer. "We are neighbors, and I'd much rather lose my garden than your friendship."

Later that night, there was a knock at the door of this kind farmer. When he opened the door, there stood his neighbor with the money he had received for damages a few days before.

Handing over the money, he said, "Please take the money back. You have something I don't have, and I want it. I want to find that kind of unselfish spirit, and maybe this will get me started!"

Now, that's what it means to turn the other cheek—to *not retaliate!* This does not mean we must be passive or namby-pamby. It does not mean weakness. On the contrary, it means strength. Any of us can lose our temper. Any of us can be selfish. Any of us can hit back. We can demand our "pound of flesh," but it takes a special person, a special spirit, a special strength to respond positively and lovingly. The Christian disciple never retaliates.

Don't Resent.

There is nothing more crippling or devastating to our spiritual lives than resentment. There is nothing that can make us sadder more quickly than resentment. There is nothing that can make us more miserable than resentment. Ovid was right when he said that resentment and envy are the meanest of vices, which creep on the ground like serpents.

In *The Gospel of Matthew,* this is where William Barclay puts the emphasis. He points out that when Jesus tells us to turn the other cheek,

> there is far more here than meets the eye, far more than a mere matter of blows on the face. Suppose a right-handed man is standing in front of another man, and suppose he wants to slap the other man on the right cheek, how must he do it? . . . *With the back of his hand.* Now according to Jewish Rabbinic law to hit a man with the *back* of the hand was twice as insulting as to hit him with the *flat* of the hand. . . . So, then, what Jesus is saying is this: "Even if a man should direct at you the most deadly and calculated insult, you must on no account . . . resent it." (vol. 1, p. 164)

Now, not too many of us are slapped around physically, but time and time again, life does bring us insults. The true Christian has forgotten what it is to be insulted. When we begin to think, "Should I be personally offended by what this person has said or done?"—at that moment, we have departed from the Spirit of Christ. As Christians, we learn from our Master how to accept any insult and never resent it, but to turn the other cheek and go on with life.

Don't Quit.

When some person, or life itself, hurts us or knocks us down, we can respond in any of several different ways:

- We can try to get even, demanding our pound of flesh.
- We can build a thick, protective shell and try to hide behind it.
- We can quit on life and try to run away.
- Or we can turn the other cheek—that is, we can get back up, dust ourselves off, stick out our chins, and go on living creatively and confidently.

The phrase "stick out your chin" means "don't quit, stand firm." I wonder if that phrase came originally from this command of Jesus to turn the other cheek.

Obviously, "turning the other cheek" does not mean that we should stay in a situation where we suffer physical or emotional abuse. When we get out of dangerous, destructive, abusive situations, we are not quitting. Turning the other cheek does not mean we should become doormats for someone else's emotional sickness. Rather, Jesus' words here mean, "Don't give up, don't become codependent, don't quit on life."

I recently saw a cartoon that made me chuckle. A little boy about six years old was sitting in a corner, obviously being disciplined by his parents. He turns his head just slightly and mutters: "Outside, I may be sitting down, but inside I'm standing up!" Maybe that's what it means to "turn the other cheek"—to have the kind of spirit that will not quit.

Have you heard the true story about a young Christian woman who was arrested because she dared to stand up for her faith? She was put in solitary confinement in an antiquated cell, with no windows and only a single light bulb, hanging on a cord in the middle of the room. She was harassed and vilified by her captors day and night.

Then one night the jailer shot out the lone light bulb, leaving her in total darkness.

"Now we have taken away your light," he cackled through the darkness. "Now what will you do?"

With courage and firmness, she answered, "You cannot take away my light. God is my light, and because he is with me, I will never be in darkness!"

That's also what it means to turn the other cheek—to stick out your chin, to trust God and refuse to quit.

Love Is the Most Powerful Thing in the World.

Love is even more powerful than physical force.

When you stop and think about it, this verse about turning the other cheek is a summary of Jesus' life. From the outset, he was the victim of all kinds of hurts—insults, lies, gossip, prejudice, slander. He was cursed and maligned, beaten and stripped, and spat upon. He was nailed to a cross, and yet *he never retaliated. He never resented. He never quit.* He just turned the other cheek and kept on loving. And then when he died, the Roman centurion who had watched him through it all and felt his love, summed it up: "Truly, this was the Son of God."

And many years later, another soldier saw it too. Napoleon put it like this: "Alexander, Caesar, Charlemagne, and myself founded empires on force. Jesus Christ alone founded his empire upon love; and at this hour, millions of people would die for him."

Jesus told us to turn the other cheek. What does that mean? It means that when hurt comes, when life strikes you a hard blow, *don't retaliate, don't resent, don't quit,* and *don't forget that love is the most powerful, the most God-like thing in the world.*

What does it mean? It means, quite simply, to live in the Spirit of Christ. Won't you try that diligently for one day? If you will try to live in that spirit for one day, it will change your life forever!

5

The Sin of Spiritual Arrogance

Luke 10:25-37 Just then a lawyer stood up to test Jesus. "Teacher," he said, "what must I do to inherit eternal life?" He said to him, "What is written in the law? What do you read there?" He answered, "You shall love the Lord your God with all your heart, and with all your soul, and with all your strength, and with all your mind; and your neighbor as yourself." And he said to him, "You have given the right answer; do this, and you will live."

But wanting to justify himself, he asked Jesus, "And who is my neighbor?" Jesus replied, "A man was going down from Jerusalem to Jericho, and fell into the hands of robbers, who stripped him, beat him, and went away, leaving him half dead. Now by chance a priest was going down that road; and when he saw him, he passed by on the other side. So likewise a Levite, when he came to the place and saw him, passed by on the other side. But a Samaritan while traveling came near him; and when he saw him, he was moved with pity. He went to him and bandaged his wounds, having poured oil and wine on them. Then he put him on his own animal, brought him to an inn, and took care of him. The next day he took out two denarii, gave them to the innkeeper, and said, 'Take care of him; and when I come back, I will repay you whatever more you spend.' Which of these three, do you think, was a neighbor to the man who fell into the hands of the robbers?" He said, "The one who showed him mercy." Jesus said to him, "Go and do likewise."

In the golden days of the settling of the West, one of the major means of transportation was the stagecoach. But did you know that stagecoaches had three different kinds of tickets—first-class, second-class, and third-class? A first-

45

class ticket meant you could sit down. No matter what happened, you could remain seated. If the stagecoach got stuck in the mud, or had trouble making it up a steep hill, or even if a wheel fell off, you remained seated because you had a first-class ticket.

A second-class ticket meant that you could sit down until there was a problem, and then you had to get off until the problem was resolved. You got off, stood to the side, and watched somebody else fix the problem. When the situation was corrected, you could get back on the stagecoach and take your seat again, because you had a second-class ticket.

A third-class ticket meant that you could sit down until there was a problem, and then you had to *get off and push!* You had to put your shoulder to it and help solve the problem, because you had a third-class ticket.

My friend Bill Hinson gave me this information, which he had seen in a Louis L'Amour novel, and as I thought about it recently, I realized that these are precisely the ways various people relate to the church. Some think they have a *first-class ticket,* and they just sit there and expect to be catered to, waited on, pampered. Others think they have a *second-class ticket,* and they ride along until there is a problem. Then they become detached spectators. They get off, stand to the side, and watch somebody else fix it.

Still others (and thank God for them) think they have a *third-class ticket.* They ride along until something goes wrong, and then they get off and push! They address the problem creatively, they work on the situation productively, and they help to fix it. They devote their energies to the immediate task of solving the problem. They roll up their sleeves and get the job done.

Now, these three ways of relating to the church are really not new. They are as old as the Bible itself. In fact, they were so pronounced in the time of Jesus that one of his most famous parables addressed that very situation. That is what the parable of the good Samaritan is all about.

The priest and the Levite in the story thought they were privileged. They didn't want to get their hands dirty. They didn't travel "tourist," much less third-class. They were important people, and they didn't need to get smudged up by the problems of the world. "Let someone else see to it"—that was their motto.

But the good Samaritan realized that he had a third-class ticket, so when he encountered the problem, he knew exactly what he was supposed to do. He got off and helped solve the problem, put his shoulder to it and brought healing, rolled up his sleeves and went to work. That's what third-class ticket-holders do. They don't mind dealing with the difficulty. They don't mind getting their hands dirty. They don't mind taking a risk or getting involved. That goes with the territory when you have a third-class ticket.

That's what made the good Samaritan "good," wasn't it? It was indeed his goodness! He was willing to help, anxious to heal, eager to serve, ready to love! He was bold enough to deal with the problem in a creative, redemptive way. He didn't just sit there and let someone else see to it. He didn't just stand off to the side and critique the way others were dealing with the difficulty. No! He felt responsible, and he addressed that troublesome situation lovingly in the spirit of Christ. And that's why, to this day, we call him the *good* Samaritan. Third-class ticket-holders are indeed good people to have around.

Jesus taught us that in this parable, and also in many other places. Again and again he said it: Those who act privileged will be last, but those who serve will be first! Those who rush to the front and act exalted will be called down, but those who are humble servants will be lifted up. He was saying, I am among you as one who serves—go and do likewise. That was the mind-set of Jesus. Time and again, we hear him saying this, and we see him doing it. Remember that earlier he had gone into the wilderness to think through the meaning of his life and the method of his ministry? What kind of Messiah would he be? That was the question he was grappling with! And he was tempted to claim a first-class ticket, to go the route of power and pleasure and privilege. But *no!* He chose instead the way of the suffering servant. He chose a third-class ticket!

Having made that choice, he went directly to the synagogue and read aloud to the people the verses from Isaiah that were to become the theme of his life: "The Spirit of the Lord is upon me, because he has anointed me to preach good news to the poor . . . release to the captives . . . sight to the blind . . . to set at liberty those who are oppressed."

Now, what was he saying? Simply this: No privileged seat for me! I have accepted a third-class ticket! And now I'm going to tackle these hard problems!

In the life and ministry of Jesus, we see something very important—that God gives us *first-class love,* but a *third-class ticket.* When trouble comes, when difficulties arise, when problems emerge, we must get off and push, we must roll up our sleeves and go to work if we want to live in the Spirit of Christ. Now, let's look at these three mind-sets, these three ways of relating to the church. And we may find ourselves somewhere between the lines.

The First-class Ticket Mind-set

Some folks in the church act as though they have first-class tickets. They expect to be catered to and waited on: "Let someone else do the dirty work, not me!"

As we know, the largest McDonald's restaurant in the world is in Moscow, the capital city of Russia. It seats more than seven hundred people. Projections are that this one restaurant will bring in approximately $15 million this year. If you will pardon the pun, the Russian people are rushing to McDonald's for a "Bolshoi Mac"!

Now, it's interesting to me that many of the Russian

people who have already dined under the golden arches in Moscow say that it's not the Western food that impresses them so much, but the way the employees cater to them:

- May I help you?
- What can I do for you?
- What would you like?
- May I serve you?
- Please enjoy your meal!
- Have a nice afternoon.
- You deserve a break today.
  —All said with a lilt in the voice
  and a warm caring smile.

In this country, we *expect* to be pampered like that when we go to a restaurant, and if we are not treated with excellent service, we are disappointed. It's part of what we call our "cater culture," and that's fine.

However, we must be careful not to let that cater-culture mind-set cloud our understanding of the real purpose of the church. We join the church to become God's servant people, not God's privileged people; God's work force, not God's pampered people.

I once read about a man who told his wife that he was physically unable to work around the house anymore, so she sent him to the doctor.

After giving the man a complete physical, the doctor told him the result: "Well, in plain English, there is nothing wrong with you. You're just lazy!"

The man thought for a moment, then said, "Could you give me a medical term for that, so I can tell my wife?"

I've thought of a great sermon title I haven't used yet, but it seems to fit here: "Are You Standing on the Promises or Just Sitting on the Premises?" Some people relate to the church with this mind-set. They sit lazily on the premises, because somehow they have the mistaken notion that they have a first-class ticket! So they just sit there and expect somebody else to do the work.

The Second-class Ticket Mind-set

Some folks relate to the church as though they have a second-class ticket. They ride along, enjoying the journey, until some difficulty or problem arises. Then they bail out, stand to the side, become detached spectators. Now, while they stand there watching others work to solve the problem, there is an added temptation—the temptation to become a Monday-morning armchair quarterback, to criticize the way the situation is being handled:

• They're doing that all wrong!
• Would you look at that?
• That group couldn't organize a two-car parade!
• If you ask me, I wouldn't do it like that!

That's the way the spectator mind-set works. They stand and watch, talk and critique, but they don't help! Like the priest and the Levite, they move quickly to the other side, thinking it is not their responsibility to address the problem.

"I don't want to get involved, so I'll stand aside and wait until somebody else fixes this."

But that is not the Christian response to trouble! That is not the way our Lord taught us to deal with difficulties. As a matter of fact, that way of relating to the church and to life is, at best, not helpful; at worst, it's even *dangerous*.

As you know, many classic pieces of literature came out of the terrible days of the Holocaust. The words of Dietrich Bonhoeffer, Anne Frank, Viktor Frankl, and other great people of faith have moved and inspired millions all over the world. Do you remember that poignant and wonderful piece written by Martin Niemoeller? Niemoeller, a German Lutheran pastor, was arrested by the Gestapo and sent to Dachau concentration camp in 1938. Amazingly, he survived the prison-camp experience and was set free by the

Allied troops in 1945. Out of that horrible experience, Niemoeller wrote these haunting words:

I DIDN'T SPEAK UP . . .

In Germany, the Nazis . . . came . . . for the Jews, and I didn't speak up because I wasn't a Jew.

Then they came for the trade unionists, and I didn't speak up because I wasn't a trade unionist.

Then they came for the Catholics, and I didn't speak up because I was a Protestant.

Then, they came for me . . . and by that time there was no one left to speak up for me.

The point is clear—we can't bail out or run away. We can't detach ourselves and stand to the side. We can't ignore the troubles of the world. We can't just wait around, expecting others to roll up their sleeves and correct the situation for us. If we are to live in the spirit of Christ, we must face our problems and deal with them redemptively.

The Third-class Ticket Mind-set

In our families, in our businesses, in our nation, and especially in our church, we need people who are willing to work, anxious to help, ready to love, eager to serve. We need people who are determined to be part of the *solution* rather than part of the *problem*. We need people who are quick to "get out and push" when we are stuck in the mud.

When a minister friend was talking to a man about joining the church, the man said, "I want to join the church because I want to be fed."

The minister answered, "Well, that's fine, but we all would be better off if you would take off your bib and put on an apron!"

Well, where do you stand? What kind of ticket are you holding right now? The Scriptures make it clear, through the life and teachings of Jesus Christ, that God does indeed give us a *first-class love,* but he also gives us a *third-class ticket!*

6

The Sins
That Are Deceptive

Luke 11:37-44 While he was speaking, a Pharisee invited him to dine with him; so he went in and took his place at the table. The Pharisee was amazed to see that he did not first wash before dinner. Then the Lord said to him, "Now you Pharisees clean the outside of the cup and of the dish, but inside you are full of greed and wickedness. You fools! Did not the one who made the outside make the inside also? So give for alms those things that are within; and see, everything will be clean for you.

"But woe to you Pharisees! For you tithe mint and rue and herbs of all kinds, and neglect justice and the love of God; it is these you ought to have practiced, without neglecting the others. Woe to you Pharisees! For you love to have the seat of honor in the synagogues and to be greeted with respect in the marketplaces. Woe to you! For you are like unmarked graves, and people walk over them without realizing it."

Some years ago, a noted evangelist announced over nationwide television that there are, by actual count, 577 different sins that people commit. That evangelist received hundreds of letters from people all over the country who wanted the list. Maybe they were afraid they might miss some! Usually, when we hear the word *sin,* we find ourselves thinking of some overt, blatant, sordid act—murder, robbery, sexual promiscuity, drunkenness. However, the truth is that we have more trouble with the "gray" sins than with the "scarlet" ones.

Those so-called little sins, which don't seem so significant at the time, those little sins that are so easy to rationalize or excuse—those are the real threats to us. They can so quickly do us in and tear us apart.

Jesus sensed this, and some of his major teachings deal with these sins that seem little—but aren't. Sins of the temperament, the attitude, the disposition. Sullenness, resentment, jealousy, envy, pettiness, arrogance, bad temper—how prevalent they are! And how much harm they do!

In Jesus' great parable of the prodigal son, the younger brother represents the "scarlet" sins of passion, and bad as those sins were, he did come home again.

But the elder brother represents the "gray" sins of temper or disposition. With the prodigal home, the house lit up, happy music in the air, dancing and feasting, the celebration going on—the elder brother, filled with anger and resentment, will not participate. That kind of attitude, that kind of little sin, keeps some people more hopelessly out of God's house than do the scarlet sins of passion.

A fascinating episode in the eleventh chapter of Luke is about this emphasis on the need for inner cleansing. There Jesus has finished speaking to a large crowd, and a Pharisee who has been listening invites him to dinner. Jesus goes home with him, sits down, and immediately begins to eat—without the ritual of washing his hands! The Pharisee is astonished—indeed, *aghast* may be more descriptive! Jesus senses this and says, "You Pharisees clean the outside of the cup and of the dish, but inside you are full of greed and wickedness. You fools! Did not the one who made the outside make the inside also? So give for alms those things that are within; and see, everything will be clean for you."

Let me rephrase the last part of that verse. Quite simply, it means that if all things within us are done in love, then naturally, everything else will be clean as well. Or to put it the other way around, if our innermost attitudes are unclean, then everything we do or say is tainted!

Now, I don't know if you noticed this or not, but this is not much of a conversation. It's pretty one-sided; the Pharisee may not have uttered a word. All of us are aware that conversation occurs on many different levels, and it is not always verbal. The hands have a language of their own. We can communicate also with our eyes and with our bodies. We may communicate joy or sorrow, amusement or horror, compassion or disdain, just by the way we stand, or sit, or fold our arms, or lift an eyebrow.

The current emphasis on body language is not really new. All my life, I have heard that what people do speaks so loudly that we can't hear what they are saying! That, I would guess, is what is working here in Luke 11. The Pharisee, although he doesn't speak, evidently makes it plain that he is disappointed in Jesus because Jesus neglected the ceremonial handwashing. This is like inviting the preacher home for Sunday dinner and seeing him sit down and begin to eat without saying grace.

At any rate, Jesus responds by telling the Pharisee that it is not consistent to be worried about external cleansing, when inwardly, he is filled with wickedness and greed. Now these are strong words.

I don't know how you feel about this, but it is clear here, as in many other places in the Bible, that Jesus is vitally concerned about the inner life, the temperament, the disposition—our innermost attitudes.

Again and again, he stresses that it's not enough to be outwardly clean. It's not enough to talk a good game. It's not enough to go through the motions. The real battlefield is within us.

A few years ago, a barbers' supply group at a convention organized a publicity stunt. They went to Skid Row and brought back the dirtiest and most helpless drunk they could find. They presented him on stage and let everybody see him.

Then they took him out and cleaned him up. They shaved him. They shampooed and styled his hair. They sprayed him with cologne. They washed him with a new kind of soap they were trying to sell. They bought him a new suit, a new shirt, tie, and shoes. And he looked great! Then they brought him back on stage to show him off, saying to all the world, "This is what our barber supplies can do for you."

But the next day, when they looked for him again, they found him right back on Skid Row—lying in the gutter, filthy and drunk!

The point of that story is obvious. It's not enough just to clean a person up on the outside. The only lasting way to be made clean is from the inside out. We must attack those seemingly "little" sins on the inside. Those are the ones that, although they may seem harmless at the time, are most likely to cut us off from God and from people. We could list all those 577, but for now, let's zero in on three that are especially dangerous: ingratitude, pride, and resentment.

Think First of Ingratitude.

Spiritually speaking, ingratitude is as debilitating to our souls as anything I can think of. This was part of the prodigal son's problem. He wasn't grateful for what he had. There was no thanksgiving in his heart, no appreciation for his father, no gratitude toward his brother, and that ungrateful disposition almost ruined him.

We read that later, "He came to himself!" Isn't that another way of saying, "He remembered his home and his father, and he discovered the spirit of gratitude"?

Gratitude is important because it reminds us of who we are and whose we are—of our need for God and our need for one another. The importance of gratitude is underscored dramatically in Thomas Gaddis' *The Birdman of Alcatraz*, which later was made into a movie starring Burt Lancaster. It is the true story of the convicted criminal and two-time murderer, Robert Stroud, a man who spent most of his seventy years behind bars and in solitary confinement.

For the first twenty years of his imprisonment, Robert Stroud was withdrawn, bitter, hostile, hard to handle. But then something happened. One day as Stroud was exercising in the prison courtyard, he found a tiny sparrow that had fallen from its nest. Stroud's first impulse was to step on the sparrow and kill it, just as he had snuffed out human life. But he didn't, because suddenly he felt something that he had not felt for many years—compassion. He picked up the bird tenderly, carried it to his cell, and gently nursed it back to health. His interest was aroused, and he read everything he could find on the subject of birds. Other prisoners brought sick birds to him, and he nursed them back to health; he discovered new cures. Before long, Robert Stroud, the dangerous, hostile, hardened criminal, became a quiet, serious, respected authority on birds.

His rehabilitation began shortly after he found that first fallen sparrow. Stroud had asked the prison guard for the orange crate on which the guard sat, so he could make a cage for the sparrow.

The guard answered, "Why should I give you this crate, Stroud? For twenty years I've tried to get through to you, and you never gave me the time of day!" But after a few minutes of silence, the guard had a change of heart and slipped the orange crate into the cell.

When Robert Stroud saw the crate, he looked up at the guard, and for the first time in twenty years, he felt gratitude. Then he said something he hadn't said in all those years—"*Thank you!*"

And that was the moment his rehabilitation began. Like the prodigal son, he had "come to himself"! He now realized his indebtedness to others, that he too needed help; that he was not the isolated, self-sufficient, independent character he had pretended to be.

In the same way, it is only when you and I can say, "Thank you," and mean it, that we begin to understand who we are and whose we are. Only when the ugly feeling of ingratitude gives way to the spirit of thankfulness, do we begin to capture the Spirit of Christ.

A part of Jesus' greatness was that wonderful attitude of appreciation, which we see especially in his thanksgiving for little things—a cup of cold water, flowers, grass, a broom, a lamb, leaven, candles, bread, fish, little children—all these spoke to him of the goodness of God. That attitude of gratitude is our calling. Any ingratitude is a virus in our souls which infects and poisons everything we do or say or touch. Ingratitude may seem harmless, but it can absolutely devastate your life and the lives of those around you.

Then Think of Pride.

Arrogant, self-centered pride is another sin that seems little—but isn't. It too can ruin your life.

I had a seminary professor who said that there are lots of little sins that are expressions and symbols of the one big Sin—the only sin with a capital letter. According to him, that one big Sin, which prompts and produces all the others, is the worship of self rather than of God. As someone put it: "Take the I out of sin, and it isn't even a word!" This arrogant pride, my professor said, is the most prevalent and worst form of idolatry.

- It's the prodigal son, saying, "I don't want to answer to my father anymore. I want to be Number One! I want to be the master. I want to be the Lord of life."
- It's Adam and Eve, saying, "Who does God think he is, telling us what we can eat and what we can't? We'll show him! We'll do what we want to do. We'll eat this fruit, and we will be as smart as God—we will be as God!"

You see, this is the fundamental problem: We are created to live as God's children, to make God the center of our lives. Instead, we want to play the part of God ourselves.

Sin, then, in other words, is expressed most dramatically in the attitude of rebellion. We rebel against God. We want to run the show. Let's transpose that into our own lives, and see if this is not indeed our story and our problem. How long has it been since you said or heard something like this:

- My life's my own—nobody's gonna tell me what to do!
- I'll do as I please.
- What's in it for me?
- You gotta look out for Number One.
- I know what I want—and nobody's gonna stop me.

Nothing can cut us off from God and from other people more quickly than this kind of arrogant pride. In *Reshaping the Christian Life,* Robert Raines put it like this:

> Hell is total preoccupation with self. Hell is the condition of being tone deaf to the word of grace, blind to the presence of God, unable to discern His image in another person. Hell is that state in which we no longer catch the fragrance of life . . . when the taste buds of life are so dulled that there is no tang or sparkle to living. Hell is to live in the presence of love and not know it, not feel it, not be warmed by it. It is to live in the Father's house like the older son (Luke 15) but be insensitive to the Father's love. Hell is to be unaware of God's world, God's people, the reality of God in oneself; it is to have the doors in life closed tight, to abide in one's own darkness. (p. 80)

If that's what hell is, then heaven must be a loving, humble openness to God and to other people. Heaven must be the embracing of God and other people—and that's tough to do when we are stuck on ourselves. One of the biggest problems we have today is the sin of arrogant *pride*.

Last, Think of Resentment.

Remember the elder brother and what happened to him. His resentment of his brother cut him off from his father. It made him miserable, and it kept him out of the party. Resentment is like that. It taints everything.

Some years ago, our family went away for a short trip. We were gone for only three days, but while we were out of town, the electricity went off. We had a turkey in the freezer section of our refrigerator, and when we returned and opened the door into the kitchen, we knew immediately what had happened. That turkey had spoiled, and the horrible odor had permeated everything. We had to throw away everything in the refrigerator—even the ice-cube trays. The stench of that spoiled turkey saturated everything.

I thought to myself, resentment is like that in our souls. It literally permeates the spirit and poisons the soul.

Now, let me say something with all the feeling I have within me: If today—at this moment—you have resentment in your heart toward anyone, don't go to sleep tonight until you have asked for God's forgiveness, until you have asked for the cleansing that only God can give. If you are angry with anyone, if you feel resentment, or hostility, or envy toward anyone; if you are bitter, if you are holding a grudge, *set it right today!* If you need to say, "I'm sorry"; if you need to say, "Thank you"—don't wait any longer! Go take care of that! Go and make it right. You see, resentment, pride, ingratitude—these are *not* little sins. They may seem harmless when compared to the more scarlet sins. They may seem small and insignificant, but let me tell you—*they are as big and as deadly as they come!*

7

The Sin
of Overreaction

Matthew 13:24-30 He put before them another parable: "The kingdom of heaven may be compared to someone who sowed good seed in his field; but while everybody was asleep, an enemy came and sowed weeds among the wheat, and then went away. So when the plants came up and bore grain, then the weeds appeared as well. And the slaves of the householder came and said to him, 'Master, did you not sow good seed in your field? Where, then, did these weeds come from?' He answered, 'An enemy has done this.' The slaves said to him, 'Then do you want us to go and gather them?' But he replied, 'No; for in gathering the weeds you would uproot the wheat along with them. Let both of them grow together until the harvest; and at harvest time I will tell the reapers, Collect the weeds first and bind them in bundles to be burned, but gather the wheat into my barn.' "

Much of the misery in the world today is caused by hasty, explosive overreaction. Friendships are destroyed, marriages are disrupted, churches are split, wars are started, lives are lost, hearts are broken, due to impulsive overreaction. If a problem presents itself, and someone facing that problem overreacts to the point of overcorrection, the result is worse than the original problem. Let me illustrate this with a few vignettes.

Some months ago, a friend of mine was driving alone down a country road. As she came out of a curve heading toward a bridge, she drove into a nightmare experience that only a great faith and tenacious determination enabled her to survive. As she rounded the curve, her right front wheel struck a bad place in the road, forcing the car onto the right shoulder and out of control. Frightened, as anyone would have been, she jerked the steering wheel hard to the left, but she had overcorrected. The car swerved back across the road, sideswiped the end of the bridge, and catapulted eighty feet through the air into the creek, landing with the front wheels on the opposite bank, the rest of the car submerged in the water.

With water up to her shoulders, a broken arm, broken ribs, a fractured neck, facial cuts, and crushed legs, she struggled to keep her head above water. She waited for what must have seemed like an eternity and prayed with all her might. Over an hour later, help finally arrived. She not only survived that terrible ordeal, but became an inspiration to all who know her.

Isn't that an interesting parable for life? It is so easy when we are under pressure to overcorrect, to overreact, and sometimes the real dangers are in the overreaction.

Recently I read about a woman who taught a third-grade Sunday school class in a United Methodist church. In her class were twin girls who seemed happy and never missed church or Sunday school. The twins came from a poor family, and their dresses were worn and out of style, but it didn't seem to bother them. But the Sunday school teacher, concerned about the twins, took up some money and bought the girls some beautiful new dresses. The next Sunday, the twin girls were missing. The teacher called their home immediately to see if they were sick.

"Oh, no, they are not sick," explained the mother. "They just looked so nice in their new dresses that I sent them to the Presbyterian church." I guess our overcorrections can come back to haunt us.

Then there was young Mary O'Connor, a devout Catholic, who fell in love with John Jones, a staunch Baptist.

They wanted to get married, but Mary's mother objected to her Catholic daughter marrying a Protestant.

Young Mary was heartbroken, but her mother suggested a solution: "Sell him on the Catholic Church," she said. "Tell him abut our sacred traditions; tell him about our long history and great beliefs. Tell him about our dedicated martyrs and noble saints. Persuade him to become a Catholic, and then you can marry him."

So Mary dried her eyes and went to see John. A little later, she returned home and burst through the door sobbing.

"What's the matter?" her mother asked. "Couldn't you sell him?"

"Sell him?" Mary cried. "I oversold him, and now he wants to become a priest!" Here we see it again—the dangers of overreaction.

We have seen this point proved a hundred times in old westerns: A man suspected of wrongdoing is put in jail to await trial. The judge has to come from Dodge City, a three-day journey. But some of the townspeople can't wait. They want their town purged of evil right now, even though the evidence against the man is not conclusive. They quickly condemn the man, organize a lynch mob, and march to the jail with torches and a rope to string up the suspect.

But the sheriff holds them off. He tells them they can't do this; they can't take the law into their own hands; they can't condemn this man to death without a fair trial; they have no conclusive evidence and no right to kill this man.

The sheriff says, "Be patient! Trust the courts! Wait for the trial. Only the judge and jury have the right to determine whether the man is guilty. Be patient. Justice will be served and righteousness will prevail."

Of course, you remember that almost every time, it turned out that the mob was wrong. The suspect was innocent, and the townspeople were embarrassed by their hasty explosive overreaction.

One of Jesus' "kingdom" parables in Matthew's Gospel underscores the danger of overreaction. It is the parable traditionally called the parable of the wheat and the tares, or the weeds among the wheat. Jesus is calling for patience, warning us against hasty, emotional, impulsive, violent action. "Be patient! Trust God! Trust the test of time! The truth will come out."

Jesus said that the kingdom is like a man who had sown his field with wheat, being very particular about the good quality of the seed. But during the night, his enemy came and sowed weeds among the wheat, then slipped away in the darkness. Later, when the servants went into the field, expecting to find a good crop, to their amazement, weeds were growing among the wheat.

They came back and asked the master, "Sir, did you not sow good seed? Where did the weeds come from?

He answers, "An enemy has done this!"

The servants, filled with anger, impulsively want to act immediately and violently. They want to purge the field. They want to rip up the weeds and get rid of them.

But the master is a man of patience and self-control. He says, "No, let's wait, for if you pull up the weeds now, you might harm the wheat. We will wait. Let both grow together, and I will separate them at the harvest. Then we will get rid of the weeds and gather the wheat into my barn."

Now, several interesting observations can be gathered from this fascinating parable: (1) There are no perfect situations; there are always weeds among the wheat. (2) The Master is not responsible for the weeds. He sowed only the best seed, but somehow we have cultivated weeds rather than the bread of life. (3) Christians are not called to be vigilantes, impulsively ripping up weeds. Rather, we are called to cultivate good wheat and trust God for the harvest. (4) There are some judgments we are not capable of making. They belong to the Master. (5) Wheat and weeds may look alike at first, but they are ultimately distinguished by their fruits. (6) The test of time is so helpful and important in the discovery of real truth. (7) There is good news here. There will be a harvest. The weeds will not choke out the wheat. So be patient, sow good seed, and trust God.

All those observations are important. In fact, each is a sermon in itself. But I want to zero in on another element in that parable—the danger of overreacting. Jesus seems to be warning us: "Don't overreact, don't overcorrect. Be patient, give it time. Keep your balance." Overreaction can be dangerous.

Overreaction Can Cause Us to Lose Our Temper.

In my opinion, loss of temper is always *over*reaction. I cannot remember a single time in my life when I lost my temper and later felt good about it. In my experience, loss of temper always has been followed by remorse and guilt and shame.

Some years ago when our daughter, Jodi, was a baby just a few months old, my wife went shopping one Saturday morning and left me home to baby-sit. It was the first time I had kept our new daughter all by myself. I put her on the floor in one of those plastic infant seats and started to read. (I had already decided that my daughter would not ever fall down or be hurt in any way; I would always be there to see that she was provided for and protected.) But I was so interested in my book, I didn't notice that she was leaning up and out of the infant seat, rocking forward.

All of a sudden she toppled out, face forward onto the hardwood floor, screaming and crying. I was startled, frightened, worried, frustrated, scared, and mad at myself. I threw my book aside and, in my haste to correct the situation, I ran right over and accidentally stepped on her hand. That hurt her worse than the fall; it hurt me worse, too.

Temper is like that, isn't it? It is an overreaction that

erupts out of frustration, fear, guilt, and unhappiness with yourself. And it always makes matters worse; it hurts everybody involved. Let Scout leaders or ministers lose their temper one time, and it is once too often. Overreaction is dangerous.

Overreaction Can Cause Us to Lose Our Marriage.

Many divorces come about because one or both parties overreacted. In the counseling room, I often suggest to couples that there is a significant difference between *reacting* and *responding*.

For example, a wife can say to her husband, "I wish we had more time together."

Now, he has a choice: He can react, get defensive, and say, "Oh, no! Here we go again. Nag, nag, nag! That's all I ever hear! I'm out there working my fingers to the bone for our family, and all I get are complaints." That's a negative reaction, an overreaction.

But he shouldn't react. He can respond! When his wife says, "I wish we had more time together," he can respond positively: "Hey! She loves me. She wants to be with me. She wants us to be together. Isn't that wonderful? Let's see what we can do about it."

You see, the choice is ours. We can react to each other, or we can respond. But if we react too often, too much, too violently, we might lose our marriage. Making a marriage work today takes a lot of patience, a lot of trust, a lot of waiting, a lot of listening, a lot of love, and a lot of responding.

Overreaction Can Cause Us to Lose Our Church.

John Savage, a United Methodist minister in New York state, wrote his Ph.D. dissertation on why people drop out of church. He came up with some interesting findings.

He discovered that only about one-third of all church members are real dropout candidates. These are people who do not handle stress well and tend to run when it appears. They drop out when some problem arises. It is almost always a misunderstanding, and it is almost always that persons's overreaction to a small problem.

Dropouts will either blame others for the problem or turn it within and blame themselves. Dropouts may suspect they are overreacting, so they "sit in the window" for a while—they stop coming to see if anyone notices, hoping someone will notice and invite them back. If no one notices, the problem is confirmed as a big one. They then go out and reorganize their activities around something else.

Now, let me express something to you as strongly as I can. Please don't let that happen to you. Don't let your feelings be hurt. Don't feel neglected. Don't let some little problem that really doesn't matter ruin your life. Don't overreact and lose your church. If you are in church, stay there. If you've dropped out, come back. Or if you've never been in the church, there's no better time than now. Overreaction is dangerous because it can cause us to lose our temper, our marriage, our church.

Overreaction Can Cause Us to Lose Our Spiritual Balance.

There are two sides to this coin. On the one hand, there is the young man brought up in the conservative home who goes off on his own for the first time and overreacts to his new freedom: "Anything goes. I can do anything I want!" That is not freedom, and we can only hope he finds his balance before he ruins his life.

On the other side of the coin, there are people who have a religious experience; they "get religion" and then overreact to the point that they want to force their experience on everybody they meet. As a result, they drive people away. Their overreaction prevents them from doing what they want most. They want to share their faith, but they only drive people away.

Several years ago, one of our nieces was lost. She was two and a half, and was lost in the woods for more than three hours. Three volunteer fire departments, a sheriff's patrol, neighbors, and bloodhounds stormed the woods trying to find that little girl. They scared her to death! So she went into the bushes to hide from them, grew tired, and fell asleep.

Finally, two little neighbor girls said they thought they could find her, so everyone was pulled back, and the two little girls went hand in hand into the woods. In less than five minutes, they came walking back with the lost child. She was tired, confused, dirty, a little scared, but perfectly safe. Everyone had so overreacted to the situation, that they had frightened the child into hiding.

Sometimes people come on so strongly about religion that they scare others off. I once heard a woman describe her husband like this: "He has become so pompous, so arrogant, so holier than thou, that now, even when he says something that's right, he says it in such a way that it makes everybody else want to be wrong!" When will we ever learn?

If we could be proud without being prideful,
If we could be reverent without being pompous,
If we could be bright without being snobbish,
If we could be serious without being sad,
If we could be concerned without being a crackpot,
If we could be committed without being closed-minded,
If we could be pure without being prudish,
If we could be good without being "holier than thou,"
then our souls could be whole and healthy and vibrant.

When Jesus told the parable of the weeds among the wheat, he wanted to convey to his listeners, then and now, a strong message: Keep your balance! Don't overreact!

8

The Sin of Hostility

Matthew 11:12-15 "From the days of John the Baptist until now the kingdom of heaven has suffered violence, and the violent take it by force. For all the prophets and the law prophesied until John came; and if you are willing to accept it, he is Elijah who is to come. Let anyone with ears listen!"

Jesus came, and he lived, and he left the world a better place—and he suffered greatly for it! Why? Jesus had committed his whole being to kindness and compassion, yet somehow he touched a nerve that aroused bitter hostility. Why? Jesus lived a life of service and mercy, yet savage opposition arose against him, and it did not rest until he was nailed to a cross! Why? Jesus spoke words of tenderness and truth and love, yet people in authority saw him as a formidable threat and clamored to silence him! Why? What happened? Why did such venomous hostility arise against Jesus?

To begin to uncover the reason for this, let me tell you about a special play I saw one Sunday evening some years ago. Some talented young people presented this play called *Construction*. It touched me; I hope you can see it sometime. It opens with a group of people gathered in an otherworldly kind of place. They don't know where they are, or how they got there, or what they are supposed to do. They discuss this. Where are we? Why are we in this place?

What is our purpose here? What are we supposed to do? Who put us here?

At this point, they notice some building materials there, so they decide that they are meant to build something. But what? The name of the play is *Construction,* but what are they supposed to build? Someone in the group wants to build a swimming pool. Another wants to build an infirmary. Still another wants to build a clubhouse.

But then one of them says, "We are not alone here. Other people are around. I have been hearing the sound of other people. We don't know who these others are or what they are like or what they are up to, and we can't afford to take a chance. It's too risky. We need to get a *wall* up before it's too late." As they discuss this further, they become frightened and decide that the suggestion is right, that they should build a wall to protect themselves from those other people out there. So they begin to build a formidable wall!

After they have worked for some time on their wall, they look up one day to see someone coming their way—a stranger. When the stranger arrives, he tells them that he is a builder and that the one who put them there sent him to help them and that he has the blueprints—the blueprints to show them what they are supposed to build! Then he tells them that they are *not* supposed to build a wall. Rather, they are supposed to build a *bridge*—a bridge to bring people together, not a wall to shut them out.

Upon hearing this, the group is enraged. They become angry with this young builder—and suspicious. Who is this man? Who does he think he is, disrupting our plans like this? After all, our wall is almost finished.

"Wait a minute," they think. "Maybe he is a spy. Maybe he is trying to trap us." The more they talk, the more frightened they become—and mob madness takes over. In a frenzied panic, they decide that the builder is a trouble-maker, that they must silence him before this crazy bridge idea of his gets out of hand. They all charge and attack him!

At this point in the play, the lights go out, the organ swells and rumbles loudly, the group shouts hostilities—then there is complete silence and darkness. Suddenly a single spotlight comes on to reveal that the young builder has been *crucified!* The play ends as the group shrinks back in horror at what they have done.

Quietly and shamefully, one of the characters says the last lines: "We must learn; we just must learn. We can't go on crucifying the *truth* forever!"

Now this to me is a very powerful play. It's unusual but relevant for us right now, because all about us, people are still building walls—walls constructed of fear and pride and anxiety and prejudice and closed minds, walls that separate people, walls that fence some in and shut others out. We are still trying to crucify the truth!

But the good news of the play is that Jesus Christ is the young Builder with the blueprints. And he wants us to tear down our walls; he wants us to be bridge-builders!

Saint Francis of Assisi sums it all up for us in his magnificent prayer:

> Lord, make me an instrument of thy peace.
> Where there is hatred, let me sow love;
> Where there is injury, pardon;
> Where there is doubt, faith;
> Where there is despair, hope;
> Where there is darkness, light;
> Where there is sadness, joy.
>
> Oh Divine Master, grant that I may not so much seek
> To be consoled, as to console,
> To be understood, as to understand,
> To be loved, as to love,
>
> for
>
> It is in giving, that we receive,
> It is in pardoning, that we are pardoned,
> It is in dying, that we are born to eternal life.

Now, that doesn't sound so controversial, does it? And yet in the play I saw, Jesus is portrayed as a troublemaker, and a quick reading of the Gospels reveals that he did upset and disturb some people. He did indeed trouble Herod and Pilate and Rome. He disturbed the Pharisees and the Sadducees, and he upset the high priests. In the New Testament, the Christ who comforts the afflicted also afflicts the comfortable! The Christ who heals broken hearts is also the one who disturbs complacent minds and exposes narrowness, hypocrisy, prejudice, selfishness, and superficiality. He turns our world upside down. He startles and confounds and shakes us out of our prisons—and knocks down the walls that divide us.

We all have heard of Jesus' *Great Commission:* "Go into all the world and make disciples." But what got him into trouble was what we might call the Great Permission. Jesus permitted people, or set them free, to do four things which, before his time, were considered unthinkable! He opened the door to four new possibilities, and that ultimately caused him to be nailed to a cross. He said: (1) It's O.K. to forgive; (2) It's O.K. to love all people; (3) It's O.K. to think; (4) It's O.K. to speak out for others.

It's O.K. to Forgive!

The law of the day in Jesus' time was "an eye for an eye and a tooth for a tooth"! If you break my little finger on my left hand, then I must break your little finger on your left hand. I can't break two of your fingers—that would be revenge. I must do exactly to you what you did to me. That's retribution, so that justice can be served. I did not have the choice to forgive.

But Jesus introduced grace and mercy and forgiveness. Remember how they criticized him: "Wait a minute, *only God can forgive!"*

But Jesus said, *"No! You can forgive!* All of us can forgive! In fact, we ought to forgive; we ought to imitate the forgiving spirit of God in all our dealings!" And Jesus was

right! If you ever wonder, Should I forgive? remember the
picture of Jesus on the cross, saying, "Father, forgive
them." That's our measuring stick for forgiveness.

In very early times, the law of the land was revenge: "If
you do something to me, I'll get you back, and then some."
Then the Law of Moses took a giant step forward by calling
only for retribution: Do no more than was done to you.
And then came Jesus, saying, "You can forgive. It's O.K.
to forgive. Indeed, it's beautiful to forgive." But the powers
in control at that time didn't want that door opened, so they
began to plot to silence him.

It's O.K. to Love All People.

Jesus said that real love in inclusive! It is goodwill toward
all. Real love sees all people as children of God. Now this
too got Jesus into trouble. He associated with the wrong
people, questionable people—sinners, tax collectors, the
blind and the lame and the sick.

There is an interesting theological point here. The
religious leaders of Jesus' time had the mistaken notion that
when people were down on their luck, it was because they
had sinned, and this was God's judgment upon them. So
blind, lame, leprous people, and the poor were looked upon
by society as sinners, wicked people, and they were
shunned.

But Jesus didn't see those people as sinners or wicked
people. He saw them as children of God, as persons of
integrity and worth, as members of God's family, as his
brothers and sisters, and he loved them and enjoyed them.
But the authorities of that day didn't like that, and they
criticized Jesus and conspired against him.

It's O.K. to Think.

I once had a weekly television program called "Something
to Think About" which aired on one of the major network

affiliates. When we first went on the air, every week a viewer sent me a letter that said, "Jim, don't tell people to think. It's dangerous." But Jesus said it's O.K. to think. Jesus said it's O.K. to learn from and speak out of your own personal experience. As the Scriptures put it, "Jesus spoke with authority, not as the scribes and Pharisees." In Jesus' day, if you asked a scribe a question, he would not give his own opinion. He would say, "I'll go look it up," and then he would quote someone or some tradition. Not so with Jesus. If you asked him a question, he would tell a parable or tell you what he thought. Sometimes he would even say, "You have heard the tradition, you have heard that it was said of old, but now *I say to you* . . . . "

This threatened the religious leaders, and they shouted, "Now you just wait a minute. Where did you get this authority?"

Let me give you an example. Four-year-old Susanna was staying with her grandfather for the weekend. She played and played, and by the end of the day her toys were all over the den.

Being a good grandfather and wanting to teach his granddaughter to be responsible, he said to her, "Now Susanna, you're through playing, so pick up all your toys and put them away."

And she said, "No, Granddaddy, I'm tired."

Granddaddy said, "Susanna, you must get down there and pick up your toys. Now get down there right now!" Susanna didn't like that, but reluctantly and pouting, she did begin to pick them up.

Then she looked at her granddaddy out of the corner of her eye and muttered, "Just who made *you* king of the world?"

And that's exactly what the Pharisees were saying to Jesus: "Just who made *you* king of the world!" If only they had known!

Jesus was saying to them, and to us, "It's O.K. to think!"

There is a fountain of living water welling up inside you. Read the great minds, study the great historical ideas, learn the great traditions; but somewhere along the line, you and I need to ask, "What do *I* think about this?"

Jesus gave us the great permission to think, to open our minds, to communicate directly with our God—to wonder, to probe, to question, to assess, to analyze, and to decide. He gave us the freedom to think, and the authorities were threatened by that. They didn't want that door unlocked and flung open, so they connived and planned to kill him.

It's O.K. to Speak Out for Others.

Jesus said that it's O.K. to speak out for social justice! Probably more than anything else, this put him on the cross. When he came to Jerusalem, he cleansed the Temple. He felt that the Temple, the sacred place of worship, had become a den of thieves.

Josephus, the Jewish historian, tells us that at this time the Temple was exploiting the people. To obtain forgiveness, they needed to sacrifice a lamb, and the Temple was charging fifteen times the cost of a lamb in the marketplace. Also, the people had to pay the Temple tax in shekels, not in Roman coins, and the Temple charged them to change their money.

Jesus was infuriated by this. The people were being exploited at the point of their basic relationship with God. This was terribly wrong, and Jesus knew it. He decided, "I'm going to speak out against this if they kill me." And that is exactly what they tried to do. He hit them in their pocketbooks, and they hit him later with a cross.

Notice how that story ends. After Jesus cleanses the Temple, he brings the lame and blind and maimed into the temple and heals them there. This is significant because the authorities did not permit the lame and blind and maimed people to come into the Temple; they considered those people imperfect, and they felt that the wrath of God was upon them. Not so with Jesus. He says, in effect, "The Temple is not here to exploit the people. The Temple is here to bring healing to the people."

But the authorities did not like that. They did not want that door opened. When Jesus gave the great *permission*, when he said it's O.K. to forgive, and it's O.K. to love all the people, and it's O.K. to think, and it's even O.K. to speak out for others, the authorities of the day were threatened. They panicked and tried to crucify the truth.

But the point is, "When will we ever learn? We can't go on crucifying the truth forever!"

The Sin
of Presumptuousness

Luke 14:7-11 When he noticed how the guests chose the places of honor, he told them a parable. "When you are invited by someone to a wedding banquet, do not sit down at the place of honor, in case someone more distinguished than you has been invited by your host; and the host who invited both of you may come and say to you, 'Give this person your place,' and then in disgrace you would start to take the lowest place. But when you are invited, go and sit down at the lowest place, so that when your host comes, he may say to you, 'Friend, move up higher'; then you will be honored in the presence of all who sit at the table with you. For all who exalt themselves will be humbled, and those who humble themselves will be exalted."

All of us, deep within us, have what Wallace Hamilton called the drum-major instinct. We all want to be important, to assert ourselves, to achieve distinction, to lead the parade. Or as one writer put it, "We all want to play Hamlet."

Alfred Adler, one of the fathers of modern psychiatry, calls it the dominant impulse in human nature. He says this desire for recognition, this wish to "be somebody," this yearning to be significant, is our strongest emotion. I don't know if Adler is right, but I think we all would agree that this drum-major instinct is a basic and important part of our human makeup.

However, we need to watch it; it can get out of hand, it can be taken too far. We must be careful with this assertive drive, or it may become a monstrous, ruthless tyrant, an arrogant, presumptuous attitude that pushes and shoves and elbows other people out of the way.

To be presumptuous is to be arrogantly proud or overly bold, to take undue liberties. It is the opposite of humility. Sometimes people are presumptuous in their interpersonal relationships; they can be haughty, egotistical, and unappreciative, taking others for granted.

The first time I really understood the word *presumptuous,* I was a freshman in college. I was there on a scholarship, playing basketball. When I came in from basketball practice one evening, my roommate met me at the door, telling me not to be upset. Bart, an upperclassman, had come into our room, had gone through my desk, found my car keys, and had borrowed my car without asking.

I had worked two jobs all summer to save enough money to buy that car, a black 1950 Ford with a rubberized chimpanzee hanging from the rearview mirror. It was a used car, but it was my prized possession. Not only that, but he had also gone through my closet and picked out my nicest and newest shirt, one I had never worn because I was saving it for a special occasion. He left, driving my new car and wearing my new shirt!

Now, as if that weren't presumptuous enough, wait till you hear the rest of the story. When Bart returned at midnight, I noticed immediately that he had spilled a chocolate milkshake on my shirt. As he handed me the car keys, he told me that my car was on a street two miles away! He had run out of gas. He suggested that I should keep more gas in the tank!

Now, that's a dramatic example of a presumptuous attitude, and it is not a very pretty picture, is it? I have been thinking recently that it is also possible to be presumptuous in religion. This kind of presumptuous religion was expressed recently by a well-known personality whose name you would recognize.

In an arrogant tone, he said, "I believe in God, but I don't like the organized church. A man can get as much religion down on his knees in his own bedroom. When I get to heaven, Jesus will be the kind of guy I want him to be! He'll go golfing with me every day, and if he doesn't like to golf, then he can caddy for me!" That is presumptuous religion!

The presumptuous attitudes of people must have bothered Jesus greatly, because one of his most famous parables and one of his most haunting statements dealt with this kind of haughtiness. And he suggested that presumptuous people are brought down by their own attitudes.

Jesus was invited to the home of a wealthy Pharisee. The dinner was also attended by other prominent persons—lawyers, teachers of the law, high-ranking officials. Jesus had noticed before, with quiet amusement and sad dismay, the sly, scheming way the leaders worked to promote themselves. He had noticed that they loved the chief seats in the synagogue and the places of prominence at public functions. And what he had noticed before was repeated here.

When the guests were called to dinner, there was an ugly, unseemly rush toward the tables—not so much for the food, but for position at the table. The rush was for the best seats, the places of prominence.

In Eastern lands, hospitality is regarded as the most prized social virtue; the Talmud set down clear rules for its procedure. Protocol—who sits where, who comes ahead of whom—is of major importance in Oriental etiquette. The uppermost seat was reserved for the most worthy guest, who sat on the left of the host; the next most worthy sat on the right of the host; and so on, down to the last and least worthy. This often made for embarrassing situations.

And so it did here in Jesus' parable. When the scramble for seats was over and the dust cleared, the host was embarrassed to discover that his guest of honor had apparently lost out in the scramble. Instead of being in the chief seat, he had taken the last seat, the lowest place, while a self-important person was complacently occupying the seat of honor. There followed an awkward silence as the host rearranged the seating.

The presumptuous man, now red-faced, was "called down" in front of everybody, while the modest man who had refused to push and shove and elbow was "called higher": "Excuse me, my friend! You are the guest of honor. Come higher. This is the place I have for you. You belong here." Jesus used this simple occurrence as a parable of eternal truth. We almost get the impression that this may well have happened that day. If Jesus had been the guest of honor, he would not have rushed for the chief seat, but would modestly have chosen the lowest seat, while the presumptuous man was embarrassed by his own self-important boldness.

This story is in the Gospel of Luke because it underscores something much more significant than a lesson in table manners. It is an illustration of the kind of spiritual law Jesus was quick to proclaim. He looked at the man whose overeagerness to be at the top ended with his being at the bottom, and he said something like, "Life is like that. Presumptuous people ultimately are called down. People who refuse to be humble may well be humiliated. Everyone who exalts himself shall be abased, and he who humbles himself shall be exalted."

The humble attitude beats the presumptuous attitude every time. The humble spirit is much better, much more Christ-like than the arrogant, pushy, presumptuous spirit.

There is a warning here for all of us: Beware of being presumptuous—but even more, beware of presumptuous religion! Here are a few tricky, presumptuous attitudes that we need to be wary of in our faith pilgrimage.

Beware of Presuming That We Have All the Answers.

Beware of becoming arrogantly closed-minded, thinking that "my way is the only way." You see, we must keep growing, stretching, learning. We must be humbly open to new truths from God.

One time when I was in New York, I had a cab driver from Honolulu. I asked him how to correctly pronounce his state: "Is it Hawaii, or Havaii?"

He answered, "Ha-va-ii."

I said, "Thank you," and he said, "You're velcome!" Even when we think we have the answer, some new truth can give it a different slant. We must be open to new insights and new ideas.

How presumptuous it is to imagine that we have all the answers regarding God's magnificent and mysterious universe. It's like going down to the ocean and saying, "I can put it all in my pocket." God's universe is filled with mystery, and it is the height of haughtiness to close the book on truth.

That's what Jim Jones tried to do. He tried to close the book on truth. He thought he had all the answers. He thought his was the only truth, and anyone who differed from him or even questioned him was punished cruelly. And that kind of closed-mindedness led to the Guyana tragedy.

A call to discipleship is a call to grow in the faith. The word *disciple* means "learner," one who is learning the faith. Good, healthy faith is humble faith that keeps on growing. It is not content with one experience with God, or a few simplistic religious notions. Many people who fall away from the faith do so because they stop growing. When we stop growing spiritually, we begin to die spiritually.

I remember a story about a little boy who fell out of bed one night.

His father rushed in to check on him: "What happened, son?"

The boy answered, "I don't know, Dad. I guess I just fell asleep too close to where I got in!"

That can happen to us in our spiritual lives, can't it?

Presumptuously thinking we have all the answers, we can get lazy and fall asleep too close to where we got in.

When I first graduated from seminary, I went through a rather presumptuous period—I am ashamed to think of it now—when I thought I was supposed to be some kind of superpreacher, someone with all the answers. But I learned through the hard knocks of life that we are not justified by simplistic, sanctimonious answers, but by faith and a loving, gracious, merciful, compassionate, forgiving God.

That early experience, however, made me identify personally with something that happened to a young minister I'll call John. John came out of seminary ready to solve all the problems of the world. He had been trained, he had studied hard, he had been a good student, and now, as pastor in a little community, he was ready to lay religion on the people. He was ready to give his answers with a pious, religious, authoritative tone. He thought he had all the answers, was in complete control, was the answer man.

The months passed quickly by, and then one day the telephone rang in his study. The father of the board chairman had died suddenly.

As John started to their home, it suddenly hit him: "I don't know what to say. I'm their pastor, and I'm scared." He tried to recall appropriate Scripture passages to quote. He tried to think of some theological message to give these people in their hour of need. He plotted his strategy: "I'll go in, gather all the family in the living room, and quote the Twenty-third Psalm. That's what I'll do! That's the answer!"

But something happened that he hadn't counted on. When John reached the home, gathered the family in the living room, and looked at those mournful faces, he realized how much he loved these people. His heart broke with them, and he was overcome with emotion. Their hurt was his hurt, and as he opened his mouth to begin the Twenty-third Psalm, no words would come, only sobs. He burst into tears and cried so much that the family came to his side to minister to him. He was so embarrassed, so ashamed. He felt he had failed his people in their hour of need.

Shortly afterward, John was transferred to another church, and fifteen years or so passed. Then one day he ran into that board chairman. He winced as he remembered that day, but something happened that surprised him.

The man's face lit up, he ran to John and hugged him tightly: "Oh John, I'm so glad to see you. Our family loves and appreciates you so much. We miss you! We talk about you all the time. We'll never forget how you came and cried with us that day when Daddy died!"

That young minister couldn't give them any answers that day long ago, but unknowingly, he had given them something better. He had given them his love. We need to beware of presuming that we have all the answers.

Beware of Presuming That
God Should Bless Us at the Expense of Others.

A number of religious magazines come across my desk. Some of them I have ordered; others just appear. Recently I came across an article by a businessman titled, "How God Answered My Prayer." The businessman and a co-worker were being considered for the same prestigious position with their company. The man said he really wanted that job, so he prayed about it.

Just before the selection was made, the co-worker had a heart attack and was hospitalized, so he was taken out of consideration. The man writing the article said, "I got the job. That's how God answered my prayer."

How presumptuous! To imagine that God, our parent, would give one child a heart attack in order to answer the prayer of another child! We must be very careful in our prayer life that we are not presumptuous, that we don't ask God to bless us at the expense of others.

Beware of Presuming That Others Know We Love Them.

In *Fiddler on the Roof,* there is a poignant scene in which Tevye keeps asking his wife, "Do you love me?" She keeps brushing the question aside, talking of how she has lived with him for so many years.

But Tevye persists, "Do you love me?" She says that she has worked side by side with him and kept the house.

Again Tevye asks, "But do you love me?" And again she sidesteps it by reminding him that she has borne his children and raised them.

But Tevye is not satisfied. He sees his daughters growing up, courting, marrying, and now suddenly the feeling of love runs strongly within him. He wants to hear it, he needs to hear it. He wants her to say it out loud. He needs reassurance; he wants to know that it is still the same with them. He needs to hear the words "I love you."

It's presumptuous of us to assume that people know we love them and appreciate them, if we never tell them. Husband and wife live together day in and day out; surely they love each other, but has it been said lately? Father and son, mother and daughter, sister and brother, live together under the same roof. Surely they love one another, but how long has it been since it was said?

Christian friends live near each other, serve in the same church, share the same pew, sing in the same choir, study in the same Sunday school class. Surely they love each other, but has it been said, has it been expressed, has it been verbalized?

Neighbors across a backyard fence, partners across an office desk—we presume our friends know we love them and appreciate them, but still the question rings out: Has it been said? Have we told them? Have we told them *lately?*

I confess that I am guilty here. There are literally hundreds of letters I need to write, hundreds of phone calls I need to make, hundreds of thank yous I need to express, hundreds of I love yous I need to verbalize. May God forgive us!

In his *Special-Day Sermons,* William Sangster mentions William Stidger's habit of writing letters of gratitude to people who had touched his life in special ways. One went to a former schoolteacher. Her answer to him is haunting:

> My dear Willie,
> I cannot tell you how much your note meant to me. I am in my eighties, living alone in a small room, cooking my own meals, lonely and . . . lingering behind.
> You will be interested to know that I taught in school for fifty years and yours is the first note of appreciation I ever received. It came on a blue-cold morning and it cheered me as nothing has in many years. (p. 147)

Our failure to express love and gratitude to others is presumptuous, and how guilty most of us are!

Beware of Presuming That Someone Else Will Uphold the Church.

Some people want a good church, but they want somebody else to see to it! Some people want a good choir, but they want someone else to do the singing. Some want a good Sunday school, but they expect somebody else to teach the classes. Some want a good youth program, but they want someone else to cook those hot dogs and climb on the hayride truck.

What if every member of the church were exactly like *you?* What kind of church would we have? Or what if every member came as often, or as seldom, as you come? What if every member gave what you give, served as you serve? What kind of church would we have? That's worth thinking about, because we must beware of presuming that someone else will uphold the church.

Beware of Presuming That
Our Wants Are More Important Than God's Will.

Sometimes what we want and what God wants happen to be the same. But oftentimes they are not, and we need to be open to that. When Jesus was praying in the Garden of Gethsemane, he didn't want to go to the cross. He said, "Father, let this cup pass from me." But he didn't stop there. No, he went on to say, "Not my will, but thine be done." *Thy will be done!* In that classic scene, we see the perfect picture of humble religion, and it's the opposite of presumptuous religion.

The Sin of Losing Our Spiritual Balance

Mark 5:1-20 They came to the other side of the sea, to the country of the Gerasenes. And when he had stepped out of the boat, immediately a man out of the tombs with an unclean spirit met him. He lived among the tombs; and no one could restrain him any more, even with a chain; for he had often been restrained with shackles and chains, but the chains he wrenched apart, and the shackles he broke in pieces; and no one had the strength to subdue him. Night and day among the tombs and on the mountains he was always howling and bruising himself with stones. When he saw Jesus from a distance, he ran and bowed down before him; and he shouted at the top of his voice, "What have you to do with me, Jesus, Son of the Most High God? I adjure you by God, do not torment me." For he had said to him, "Come out of the man, you unclean spirit!" Then Jesus asked him, "What is your name?" He replied, "My name is Legion; for we are many." He begged him earnestly not to send them out of the country. Now there on the hillside a great herd of swine was feeding; and the unclean spirits begged him, "Send us into the swine; let us enter them." So he gave them permission. And the unclean spirits came out and entered the swine; and the herd, numbering about two thousand, rushed down the steep bank into the sea, and were drowned in the sea.

The swineherds ran off and told it in the city and in the country. Then people came to see what it was that had happened. They came to Jesus and saw the demoniac sitting there, clothed and in his right mind, the very man who had had the legion; and they were afraid. Those who had seen what had happened to the demoniac and to the swine reported it. Then they began to beg Jesus to leave their neighborhood. As he was getting into the boat, the man who had been possessed by demons begged him that he might be with him. But Jesus refused, and said to him, "Go home to your friends, and tell them how much the Lord has done for you, and what mercy he has shown you." And he went away and began to proclaim in the Decapolis how much Jesus had done for him; and everyone was amazed.

Every time we think it's safe to take a shower again, they come out with another *Psycho* movie! Remember the first one? In that film, noted director Alfred Hitchcock held us in great suspense—and scared us out of our wits! This was especially true of the classic shower scene in which Janet Leigh frighteningly met her demise. That scene so terrified us that for months and months, millions of Americans were literally afraid to take a shower.

How did Hitchcock do that? How did he reduce us to such terror that people in the theater closed their eyes, or screamed aloud, or leaped from their seats? Why, the young woman sitting next to me was shocked, amazed, and speechless. And I was terribly embarrassed as I tried to figure out how to gracefully get off her lap!

How did Hitchcock terrify us so? Well, he did it with eerie sights and sounds and scary music. Mostly though, he did it through a strange character played by Anthony Perkins, a character who was mentally, emotionally, and spiritually unbalanced. Unbalanced personalities frighten us. They terrify us, confuse us, scare us. We don't know how to respond to them.

If someone has a broken arm, a headache, or a bad appendix, we know what to do. But if someone has a sick, broken, or unbalanced mind or spirit, we throw up our hands. We don't know what on earth to do. Most of us feel threatened, undone, uncomfortable around such unpredictable people.

Unbalanced personalities always have frightened the societies in which they live. Today we have excellent hospitals with well-trained medical professionals who are doing remarkable things in the treatment of unbalanced personalities. But in the time of Jesus, there were no such hospitals, no talented medical teams, no institutions dedicated to dealing with that difficult illness. They dealt with the problem simply by casting such people out of civilized society. They were banished to desolate areas and sometimes even chained up like wild animals. Society excused this action by declaring that these unbalanced personalities were demon-possessed.

That claim was so convincing that even the sick persons involved believed it. They knew something was wrong. Their minds were mixed up. Their emotions were traumatized. The rhythm of their lives was "out of sync." They felt pulled, twisted, torn within. So they too blamed it on demons and accepted their outcast status.

Now, there is a dramatic example of this in Mark 5, in which Jesus encounters the Gerasene demoniac—a madman who, in horror-story fashion, runs shrieking out of the tombs. He is so unbalanced that he believes he is held captive by a whole legion of demons. He causes such a ruckus that a herd of pigs is thrown into a panic and stampedes into the sea.

Now, that is a perfect setup for a horror story. Just think what Hitchcock could have done with this:

- a desolate cemetery
- limestone caves and tombs
- nighttime and shadows
- a storm at sea, with waves crashing on the shore
- a shrieking madman, with strength so incredible he can't be bound or subdued
- a psycho, an unbalanced personality who thinks he is possessed by a legion of demons
- a stampeding herd of swine, squealing loudly as they plummet into the sea.

This is an eerie, grim, suspenseful, frightening situation. Jesus and his disciples have just come through a storm on the Sea of Galilee. It is nighttime.

As they get out of the boat, they hear strange sounds coming from the tombs—shrieks, growls, screams, the rattling of chains. Then suddenly—a horrifying sight! A madman with tattered clothes, bruised, bloody, and battered, with pieces of chains dangling from his arms and ankles, runs screaming directly toward them!

What would you have done? I think I would have run for my life or jumped back into the boat. But not Jesus! He stood his ground and faced the madman. He healed him—and brought peace to his troubled soul. And he convinced the man that he was now set free.

Broadly speaking, there are two kinds of medicine: rescue medicine, which seeks to correct a bad situation, and preventive medicine, which seeks to prevent the bad situation in the first place.

In this story, we see Jesus performing rescue medicine—correcting a bad situation. But what preventive measures can we take in our own lives? How can we cultivate ways to help us preserve our spiritual freedom and maintain our spiritual balance?

We Need to Keep Our Sense of Priorities.

The truth is that many people today

- worry themselves silly
- get themselves out of sorts
- drive themselves crazy over things that do
  not really matter.

We need to remember what really matters and put our energy there, weeding out all the rest. We need to get our priorities straight.

I have a friend who is an inspiration to everyone who

knows him. He is an outstanding professional, highly regarded, actively involved in his work, his church, and his community. He is a double amputee, but if you were not aware of that fact, you would never guess it. With artificial legs and a cane, he walks, works, and lives life to the full—and never complains.

Once as we were walking together, he said something I will never forget. Putting his hand gently on my shoulder, he said, "Jim, having no legs is not a problem . . . unless you let it be."

As we walked on, I felt ashamed and inspired—ashamed of the times I have felt sorry for myself or wallowed in self-pity because of some little inconvenience; inspired by that man's great spirit to get my priorities straight. If we want to be spiritually healthy people and keep our freedom and balance, we need to give our time, our energy, our creativity, to the matters that really matter. We need to keep our sense of priorities.

We Need to Keep Our Sense of Humor.

I don't know what happened to that Gerasene madman that threw him so off balance, but I do know that people with no sense of humor frighten me. Some people make themselves sick because they have forgotten how to laugh.

It concerns me that so many professional comedians these days really misunderstand humor. They are so insecure, they think that using profane language and gutter talk is the only way to make people laugh. The really great comedians know better. They know that the best humor is a good laugh at ourselves. Jack Benny, Will Rogers, and Red Skelton were great because they helped us laugh at ourselves, not take ourselves too seriously. They helped us lighten up.

Some years ago I heard of a minister who paid a great price the night he left his sense of humor at home.

He had discovered that some pastors get a whole month of

vacation, so he went to the board meeting and suggested that he, too, should be given a full month's vacation.

At this point, a friend in the back of the room said, "I heard him preach last Sunday, so I move we give him a month's vacation, and pick a month with five Sundays in it!"

Now, the man who said that really liked the minister and meant him no harm. He was only joking. But sadly, that minister had lost his sense of humor. He had forgotten how to laugh, and that night in the board meeting, he lost his temper, he lost his witness, he lost his balance, and he lost his ministry!

If we want to keep our spiritual balance, we need to lighten up and keep our sense of humor.

We Need to Keep Our Sense of the Holy Habits.

Regular church attendance, regular prayer, regular study of the Scriptures, regularly helping other people, striving daily to live the faith—all these are great spiritual vitamins that can help keep our souls healthy and our personalities balanced.

A little four-year-old boy was the ring bearer at one wedding I performed in our chapel. He was self-conscious and very unexcited about this love and marriage business. He came down the aisle tossing the ring pillow up in the air, and when he arrived at the altar rail, he promptly stretched out on the kneeling pad. Later, he stood up and walked around, waving to his grandparents. He just could not get interested in the wedding at all—until we came to the Lord's Prayer! At that point, he perked up and plugged in. For the first time, he felt comfortable. And he prayed the Lord's Prayer boldly, confidently, and loudly—louder than anybody else in the room. He really boomed it out!

I felt good about that, and I felt good about that little boy. He couldn't read or write yet, and he couldn't get excited about weddings yet, but already he knew and loved the

Lord's Prayer. Someone was teaching him the holy habits that will serve him well in the days ahead. If we want to keep our spiritual balance, we need to keep our sense of priorities, our sense of humor, and our sense of the holy habits.

We Need to Keep Our Sense of Partnership with God.

The words *holiness* and *wholeness* are closely related, and they both mean "living in harmony with God."

Not long ago one of our United Methodist colleges in the Southwest had a Career Day on Campus. I was asked to be on a panel to discuss "How Faith Influences Your Choice of a Career." At the start of the session, the panelists were asked to introduce themselves and mention their particular vocations. It was a rather routine beginning. One woman gave her name and said, "I'm an attorney." A man gave his name and said, "I'm in business. I own a computer company." The woman seated next to me indicated that she was in real estate. I was next, and I said, "I'm a minister." But on my other side was a doctor, and when his turn came, his statement changed that mundane situation into a special and sacred moment:

> "We are here today to talk about vocation. The word *vocation* means 'calling.' Well, my calling is to be a Christian . . . and one of the ways I do that is through the practice of medicine."

That was a beautiful statement, a good thing to say to those college students, and a great philosophy of life.

That doctor wasn't being pompous or arrogant. He is a humble man who has a strong sense of partnership with God. As he spoke, I found myself thinking, "The next time I get sick, I'm going to look this doctor up!"

A sense of partnership with God—that is so important. If

you and I could approach every day, every situation, with that mind-set—I'm a co-worker with God—it would change everything. It would change our temperaments, our attitudes, our perspectives. It would change our lives! The hymn-writer put it like this:

> Breathe on me, Breath of God,
> fill me with life anew,
> that I may love what thou dost love,
> and do what thou wouldst do.
>
> Breathe on me, Breath of God,
> until my heart is pure,
> until with thee I will one will,
> to do and to endure.
>
> Breathe on me, Breath of God,
> till I am wholly thine,
> till all this earthly part of me
> glows with thy fire divine.

—Edwin Hatch, 1878

Sin . . . and Redemption

Genesis 50:15-21 Realizing that their father was dead, Joseph's brothers said, "What if Joseph still bears a grudge against us and pays us back in full for all the wrong that we did to him?" So they approached Joseph, saying, "Your father gave this instruction before he died, 'Say to Joseph: I beg you, forgive the crime of your brothers and the wrong they did in harming you.' Now therefore please forgive the crime of the servants of the God of your father." Joseph wept when they spoke to him. Then his brothers also wept, fell down before him, and said, "We are here as your slaves." But Joseph said to them, "Do not be afraid! Am I in the place of God? Even though you intended to do harm to me, God intended it for good, in order to preserve a numerous people, as he is doing today. So have no fear; I myself will provide for you and your little ones." In this way he reassured them, speaking kindly to them.

Let me begin with one of the most important questions ever raised: Can people change? Can human nature be changed?

We often talk and act as if that is not possible. "She's just made that way," we say, or "He's not going to change." And then, with a note of dramatic finality, we add, "After all, a leopard can't change its spots!"

Well, a leopard may not be able to change its spots, but there is a vast difference between a leopard and a human soul!

A part of the good news of our faith is that change *is*

possible! We *can* change! When we stop to think about it, we realize that human nature may well be the one thing in this universe that can be changed. We cannot change the force of gravity. We cannot change the movement of the oceans or the stars. We cannot change any of the dependable laws of nature. But the commitments, the habits—indeed, the lives of people, have been and can be changed. It is a common experience of life.

In my opinion, that is what the word *redemption* is all about. It means that bad things can be changed to good things, bad habits can be replaced with good habits, defeats can be turned into victories, weak people can be converted into strong, courageous people.

This is precisely what this story in the book of Genesis is about. This is what Joseph meant: "God has made me fruitful in the land of my affliction." Evil was plotted against him, he said, "but God meant it for good." In other words, God redeemed the situation. God took these bad circumstances and somehow turned them into good.

In the unforgettable story of Joseph, we see a man who learned how to suffer creatively, learning through his own experience how God works to redeem things. Joseph was one of the twelve sons of Jacob—his father's favorite son. This favoritism which Joseph enjoyed—and flaunted with his aristocratic coat of many colors—didn't set too well with his brothers. They were jealous, envious, resentful, bitter. In fact, they became so hostile that they actually kidnapped him, intending to murder him. But when some slave traders came by on their way to Egypt, Joseph's brothers sold him into slavery.

You recall the rest of the story: Joseph, through his faith in God and his unique ability to interpret dreams, goes from rags to riches and eventually becomes prime minister of Egypt. Then he saves Egypt and his own family from famine and sums it all up by saying to his brothers in the spirit of forgiveness, "You meant evil against me; but God meant it for good!"

This is one of the high points of spiritual greatness in the Old Testament—indeed, in the whole Bible. Joseph shows great spiritual maturity as he is able to say, to those who had wanted to kill him, that God was able to turn even their cruel motives and shady actions into something good.

The message of this masterful story is that *God redeems!* God has the power to turn bad things into good things, weakness into strength, failure into success, defeat into victory.

God redeems. This is the good news, isn't it? It means that no failure needs to be final! We can bounce back! We can change! We can start over! We can be given a new beginning. Let me be more specific: Events can be redeemed; things can be redeemed; words can be redeemed; and finally, people can be redeemed.

Events Can Be Redeemed.

We see this graphically in the Joseph story. We see treachery, deceit, jealousy, hatred, and lies that led to kidnapping, slavery, and imprisonment. Terrible events— but God redeemed those events, brought good out of them. God often does that.

Some years ago when I was in seminary, I took a course called Pastoral Care. As part of that course, each student did some clinical work. I was assigned to the neurosurgery floor of a nearby hospital. Every Thursday I would talk with the head nurse about which patients might need a minister; then I would visit them and write reports about my visit. It was a great experience. I could help people while I learned how to be a pastor.

One afternoon the head nurse was waiting for me at the elevator: "Jim, I'm so glad you're here. Mrs. Davis needs you. She's in room 858, and she really needs a pastor today.

She is to have brain surgery in the morning, and to be honest, it's touch and go; she may not make it. On top of her terrible physical situation, we are concerned because her attitude is so bad. She is wallowing in self-pity, and she has lost her will to live. She needs spiritual help; she needs a minister. She needs you, Jim."

It scared me to death. I was uncertain, inexperienced, and terrified. I didn't know what to say to this woman who was facing critical surgery the next morning and needed spiritual help so desperately. As I turned to walk toward her room, I tried to figure out how to handle this delicate situation. Then I remembered something from the course on pastoral care—nondirective counseling.

In nondirective counseling, the counselor lets the person talk out the problems, have the catharsis of speaking them out. The counselor just grunts now and then or says, "Hmm," or repeats back what the person says. If the person says, "I feel so lonely," the counselor says, "Oh, you feel lonely." If the person says, "I feel so sad," the counselor says, "You're feeling sad today." And so on and on. And the person thanks you for this great advice you've given!

I decided this was the answer; I would use nondirective counseling with Mrs. Davis, and very confidently I began to walk toward her room. Just as I reached for the door, I heard the nurse running down the hall.

"Wait a minute, Jim. I almost forgot to tell you. Mrs. Davis is so critically ill, and this surgery in the morning is so delicate, the doctors want her completely quiet; she is not allowed to speak." There went my plan! My confidence was completely gone!

I opened the door a crack and peered inside. It was dark and bare. The draperies were drawn; no cards, no flowers, no friends. Mrs. Davis was lying in bed, very sullen; her head was shaved. The room reeked of death.

I was terrified, and in my anxiety, I did everything wrong! I pushed the door too hard and it slammed against the wall. I promptly walked over and kicked the bed. I stammered and stuttered and said all the wrong things. Finally in desperation, I tried to pray, and I botched that up! I walked out of the room embarrassed, with tears in my eyes, ready to quit the ministry. Here was a person in real need, and I had failed miserably. I was so ashamed!

A few days later, when I returned to the hospital, I rushed to the eighth floor and quickly scanned the patient list to see if Mrs. Davis had made it through the surgery. There was her name on the list: Mrs. Davis, Room 858—condition: good. I was amazed. I walked into the room and was impressed by how completely different it looked. The draperies were open and sunshine filled the room. Flowers and cards were everywhere, and Mrs. Davis was sitting up, writing letters.

"Mrs. Davis, you probably don't remember me—"

"Don't remember you?" she said. "How could I ever forget you! You saved my life!"

"But I don't understand. I felt so terrible; I was so ashamed. I did everything wrong!"

"That's just it," she replied. "I felt so sorry for you! It was the first time I had felt anything but self-pity for months. That little spark of compassion ignited in me the will to live! And the doctors tell me it made all the difference."

Isn't that something! God can take our terrible failures and redeem them! God redeems events. God takes our weakness and makes it strength, takes our defeats and turns them into victories; and that's what keeps us going. We have only to do our best and trust God to bring it out right.

Things Can Be Redeemed.

God can even redeem material things. For example, there is a Broadway musical called *Joseph and the Amazing Technicolor Dreamcoat*. When we hear that, we smile. Originally, that coat was not something to smile about; it was the symbol of favoritism that fanned the flames of jealousy. But over the years, God redeemed that "thing."

John Wesley's study desk, on display in his home in London, is another example. That same desk once belonged to a bookie. Designed originally for taking bets, it was redeemed to be a place of spiritual power, where John Wesley thought through and wrote his greatest sermons.

Luther Burbank once said that a plant born a weed need not remain a weed; so you see, peas and carrots may be nothing but weeds that have been redeemed.

In a little church in the Fiji Islands, there is an unusual baptismal font. The large stone, deeply stained, with a portion of the top hollowed out to hold water, was once called the Killing Rock, the place where cannibals brought their victims. It is now the place where they bring their babies to be baptized!

And the cross, once the emblem of suffering and shame and punishment and death, has been redeemed. Now it is the symbol of love and victory and forgiveness and life. So you see, events can be redeemed, and things can be redeemed.

Words Can Be Redeemed.

Today, with some affection, we refer to Joseph as the *dreamer,* but when he was first given that title, it was not complimentary. That's what his older brothers called him as they plotted evil against him. "Here comes the dreamer," they said mockingly, their words coated with hatred; but over the years, the name was redeemed.

The same is true of the word *Methodist.* John Wesley and his friends were first called Methodist in derision, when people noticed how methodical they were and called them tauntingly, "those methodists." But over the years, God redeemed the word.

People Can Be Redeemed.

People like Joseph's brothers, people like you and me, can be redeemed, changed, converted. We can be forgiven, reshaped, reclaimed. Let me ask you: Is there something in your life that needs to be changed? Is there a secret sin, a vengeful spirit, a bad temper, a lack of commitment, a hateful attitude that you would be a lot better off without? If you are willing, God can change you.

Occasionally I pass through a part of our city that is anything but beautiful; scrap iron, old bottles and cans, rags, wrecked cars, broken machinery are dumped there. Recently while going by, I saw great quantities of scrap iron being loaded onto a railroad car. It will go to a factory to be reclaimed, to be melted down and remade into something new. It may come out as surgeon's tools or fenders for a new car, or maybe even a steeple for a church. Who knows what it may be, but it will be new and useful and valuable.

If we can do that with our old scrap iron, how much more can God do with human beings, people like you and me. God wants to reclaim us, reshape us. God wants to redeem us!

12

Sin . . . and Grace

Luke 15:6b, 9b, 22-24 "Rejoice with me, for I have found my sheep that was lost." . . . "Rejoice with me, for I have found the coin that I had lost." . . . "Quickly, bring out a robe—the best one—and put it on him; put a ring on his finger and sandals on his feet. And get the fatted calf and kill it, and let us eat and celebrate; for this son of mine was dead and is alive again; he was lost and is found!"

Have you ever been lost? Most of you probably have been lost somewhere at some time. It is a terrible feeling, and frightening. Panic sets in quickly; you start walking fast, your eyes darting in every direction, scanning the horizon, searching frantically for any familiar sign. Then you begin to run, in the desperate hope that running will somehow help you find your way more quickly. Time seems different when you are lost, and a scant few minutes of lostness may feel like an eternity. Being lost is an awful experience!

When I was seven, I got lost at Ringling Brothers' Circus. More than twenty thousand people were there that night. My older brother Bob, who was nine, had taken me by the hand down one of the exit ramps from the arena to the crowded concession stand to get some cotton candy. There were no neat lines. People were pushing and pressing toward the counter, trying to get the vendor's attention. Since my brother was taller, the cotton-candy man saw him and served him first; Bob then stepped to the side to wait for me.

At least, he meant to wait for me. But just then loud laughter came from the arena, followed by thunderous applause and fireworks. The ringmaster's voice exploded over the public address system, introducing the clowns, the main act we wanted to see. My brother didn't mean to leave me, but the excitement was just too much for him, and he ran back up the ramp to catch a glimpse of the clowns. He meant to wait for me there, but a policeman told him he couldn't stand there and asked to see his ticket stub. When Bob fished into his pocket, he came up with two ticket stubs—his and mine, so the policeman promptly escorted him to his seat.

By this time, I had my cotton candy, and I looked toward the spot where my brother had been standing only moments before. But now he was gone, and I felt sick deep down in the pit of my stomach. I was scared to death! I was all alone in that huge crowd! I didn't know which ramp to go up; I didn't know which section our seats were in. All the ramps and entrances looked the same. I couldn't find my ticket stub, and to top it off, I had lost my appetite for cotton candy. Terrified now, I went up the wrong ramp, and when I entered the huge auditorium, I turned the wrong way!

Nothing looked familiar. I wondered if I would ever see my family again. I started to run, trying (not too successfully) to fight back the tears. Panic-stricken, I looked frantically for a familiar sign or a friendly face, but all eyes were riveted on the clowns in the center of the arena. Everyone was laughing loudly at the antics of the clowns. They weren't funny to me at that moment. I remember thinking, "How can they laugh at a time like this? How can they laugh when I feel so lost?"

Just then I felt a touch on my shoulder. I turned around, to be gathered up into strong loving arms. It was my dad. My father had come after me and had found me. It was a good thing he did, because I was running as fast as my tired, scared legs would carry me—in the wrong direction. He held me, calmed me down, reassured me, then took me downstairs and bought me a Coke, a hot dog, a Yo-Yo, a lizard, a little stuffed bear, and a candy apple. I learned a valuable lesson that day: Being lost is terrible, but being found is wonderful!

Feeling lost is one of the worst feelings I know. Did you know that some people go through life feeling lost? They feel so out of touch, rejected, cut off, estranged, alienated, so out of place. And all of us feel lost like that sometimes; when we do, it is probably a red flag, a sign that we have lost our way with God. If we don't keep our relationship with God fresh, if we don't renew our commitment to God every day, if we don't stay close to the church, if we don't spend some time in prayer, we can become lost so fast it can make your head spin!

Jesus realized this, and in the Gospel of Luke, he strings together three parables which show vividly how people are lost, and how they are found. In those three famous parables—the lost sheep, the lost coin, and the lost son—we see there are several ways we can become lost.

We Can Get Lost by Wandering Off.

We can get lost by carelessly wandering off like a lost sheep. I am sure that the little lamb in the parable did not mean to be lost; it was not its intention to separate itself from the rest of the flock and the shepherd. It just began to nibble on some grass, and it was so good that the lamb kept on nibbling with its head down, until all of a sudden it looked up, and the rest of the sheep were nowhere to be seen, and neither was the shepherd.

They didn't run off and leave it. The lamb just wandered away when no one was looking. It didn't keep in touch! It didn't mean to get lost, but that's what happens when we wander off. And it can happen in our relationship with God. We can drift away, wander off, lose contact, slide out of

104 YES LORD, I HAVE SINNED

touch. We don't mean to slip away, but carelessly, unintentionally, sometimes we do. We don't pay enough attention to our relationship with God. We don't discipline ourselves to keep the relationship fresh and vibrant and alive, and then suddenly it has grown cold, and we find ourselves lost.

Someone once defined religion as friendship with God. I like that idea: Faith is friendship with God! And we all know that friendships survive by association, by contact, by keeping in touch. The friends most real to you right now are those with whom you associate, those you spend time with!

Suppose that some years ago, you had a friend who lived next door. You worked together for the same company. You were neighbors, doing favors for each other. You enjoyed being together; you played golf together, went to church together, and watched sports events together. You were together part of almost every day, and you felt close to that person. The influence of that life on yours was real and vivid. Your friend was an important part of your life.

But then you moved to another city. At first, you kept in touch by mail and an occasional visit or long-distance phone call. But as time went by, your times together became fewer and fewer. Now you associate very little, and as a result, you have organized your life, your time, and your energies around other things and other people.

Now, you still count that person as your friend, but the influence of that life on yours is simply not as marked or as significant as it once was. If two people are to be real to each other, they must associate, they must spend time together! I'm sure there is some truth in the old saying, "Absence makes the heart grow fonder," but there may be more truth in that other saying—"Out of sight, out of mind."

Of course, the spiritual application of this principle is obvious: If we want our friendship with God to be alive and well, we must associate with God, we must stay close to

God, we must spend time with God, we must keep in touch with God.

Let me ask you. This past week, how much time have you spent with God? How many minutes have you spent with God in prayer? How many minutes have you spent with God in the study of the Scriptures? How much time have you spent with God, serving and loving God through the church with your heart, soul, mind, and strength? Like a little lamb, we can wander off and get lost.

We Can Be Led Astray by Others.

Other people, through their influence, can cause us to get lost. In the second parable, the lost coin did not sprout wings and fly away; it did not lose itself; it was not responsible for its lostness; someone else caused it. The woman lost the coin. It's as simple as that.

This reminds us dramatically of our influence upon one another. Some people can be either lost or found because of me and my influence, and because of you and your influence. What an awesome responsibility we have! On which side of the ledger is our influence coming down? Are we lighting candles so that others can find their way? Or are we blowing them out, causing people to stumble around in darkness?

A few years ago, as I watched our son Jeff play baseball, a nice-looking young man sat down beside me and struck up a conversation: "Are you Jim Moore?"

When I said I was, he continued, "You're a minister, aren't you?" But before I could answer, he went on, "You know, Jim, I've never been to a church service in my life."

"Why not?" I asked.

"Well," he said, "I had a bad experience when I was twelve years old. My family didn't go to church, and I didn't know anything about it. But I was curious, so one Saturday afternoon, I went into this church building near my home to look around. I didn't mean any harm, but while I was in there, this man came up behind me and grabbed me. He accused me of trying to steal something. He ran me out and threatened to call the police. I've never been back in a church. I guess it's unfair to judge the church by that one experience. But to this day, when I think of the church, I think of that man and the look on his face, the tone of his voice, his hateful attitude, and I shudder. I cringe inside!"

How vital it is that we in the church realize the importance of our influence on every person we meet! At any given moment, our influence—our tone of voice, our touch, the look on our face—may turn them on to the church. Or it may turn them away from the church. Some people are lost by wandering away; others are led astray by the influence of others.

The other side of this coin is that we must be strong enough to take charge of our own lives, to know our own minds, to be obedient to our commitments, so that bad influences or mixed-up people or peer pressures or current fads will not be able to tear us away from our devotion to God and the church.

We Can Get Lost by Running Away.

Sometimes we rebel and turn away from our responsibilities; we look for love in the wrong places, we look for life in the "far country" of selfishness. This was how the prodigal son was lost—arrogantly, willfully, egotistically. He grew restless and went to his father, saying he wanted to leave home: "Give me my inheritance now. I don't want to wait around until you die. I want to be my own boss, do my own thing."

When you look at the prodigal son, the descriptive adjectives fly fast and furious—*rebellious, restless, discontented, arrogant, prideful, immature, self-centered.* But all these adjectives are symptoms of something deeper! What is his sin? What is his lostness? It is simply this: Even though he is a child, he doesn't want to be a child; even though he is a brother, he doesn't want to be a brother. He rejects his father and his brother, and any time we do that, we are in the far country, because we are far from what God intended us to be. We are meant to be God's children, brothers and sisters to one another. It's hard to remember that sometimes, because each of us wants to be Number One.

One of my favorite stories was told by Bishop Gerald Kennedy some years ago. A young man was proposing marriage to his girlfriend: "I admit that I'm not wealthy like Jerome; I'm not as handsome as Jerome; I don't have a country estate or a yacht or a private plane like Jerome's. But my darling, I love you."

The girl answered, "I love you too, but tell me more about Jerome!"

Yes, we go through life crying, "What's in it for me?" or, "Tell me more about Jerome!"

This was the prodigal's problem, and that was precisely why he was lost. When we run away from our parents and desert our brother, we are lost, for we are in the far country of selfishness.

We Can Be Lost in Resentment.

Resentment was the elder brother's problem. He stayed home, but he was just as lost because of the resentment that was eating him up inside. At first glance, he doesn't seem lost. He is at home, surrounded by his family and many other people, but he may well be the most lost of all. When we survey him closely, the descriptive adjectives again fly fast and furious—*resentful, judgmental, envious, jealous, hostile, bitter, angry, self-righteous.*

He hears the joyous music coming from the house and asks, "What's going on?"

A servant answers, "Your brother has returned home,

and your father is so happy he has killed the fatted calf and called for a great celebration."

When the elder brother hears this, does he run to welcome his lost brother home? No, not quite! He becomes angry, hurt, sullen, and refuses to go inside. The father comes out to encourage him to come on in and join the celebration, but he absolutely refuses. His bitter resentment cuts him off not only from his brother, but also from his father. And it causes him to miss the party!

Remember that Jesus is telling this parable to a group of people who are self-righteous "elder brothers," people who were angry with him for celebrating life with the down-and-out poor.

Remember the old Amos and Andy radio program? In one episode, Kingfish, instead of shaking hands to greet Andy, affectionately slapped him on the chest. But this infuriated Andy, and as the show went on, Andy became more and more resentful.

At the end of the program, Andy came in with a big smile on his face and said to Amos, "I'm ready for him now, Amos. Just let the Kingfish slap me on the chest, and see what he gets."

Amos asked, "Why Andy, what have you done?"

Andy answered, "In my vest pocket, I have two sticks of dynamite. Now, when Kingfish slaps me on the chest, it's gonna blow his hand clean off!" But Andy didn't realize that it also would blow his heart right out.

That's what resentment does to us, and it's the worst kind of lostness. Some are lost by wandering off, drifting away like lost sheep. Others are lost by the influence of others, being led astray or pushed away. Still others are lost by rebelliously running away to the far country. And then some stay home, but still are lost in their bitter resentment.

These wonderful parables in Luke 15 are not merely about lostness. They are about being found. They are about a God who, like a loving parent, wants to seek us out and find us; a parent who wants to bring us back into the fold, back from the dark places, back from the far country, for the great celebration. Notice that each parable resounds with joy when the lost are finally found.

These three parables underscore what I learned the hard way at the circus when I was seven years old: Being lost feels awful, but being found by a loving parent is absolutely wonderful!

Suggestions for Leading a Study of *Yes, Lord, I Have Sinned, But I Have Several Excellent Excuses!*

Life is full of excuses. We get stuck in traffic. We are late for an appointment. We forget important dates. We have too many things going on at the same time. If we are to be honest with ourselves, our excuses creep into our lives of faith as well.

This booklet is meant to be a challenge and guide. It will offer ways to enhance your study and discussion of *Yes, Lord, I Have Sinned, But I Have Several Excellent Excuses* (James W. Moore, © Abingdon Press, 1991).

As you begin reading this book, keep in mind that people learn in a variety of ways. Some people like to learn by analyzing information in a step-by-step process; others, by visualizing information—creating a picture in the mind that represents the information that may or may not be in any order; others, by thinking more abstractly about the information. Some people may learn using a combination of these methods. People approach Bible study in different ways.

This guide is written to help you look at the biblical texts, stories, and excuses contained in each of the twelve chapters by taking into account the different ways people learn. Some questions will ask that you think logically about an issue; others, that you think emotionally about a situation. Still other questions or activities may ask you to draw or paint or sculpt something to help gain insights from each chapter.

Don't let this Bible study lead you. You lead it. Use the questions as you want. Don't feel the need to answer every question or complete every activity. If you find that one of the questions or activities leads you off into another discussion, feel free to pursue such a discussion as time and group interest allow. People will usually talk about things that interest them, so feel free to let the group journey as it will. At the same time, however, be careful that one person does not dominate the conversation. If this is a group study, the purpose is to get the entire group involved.

Leader's Guide Sections: You'll note that this leader's guide is broken down into various sections. These are to help focus the discussion and provide a guide for your study. You'll note that answers are not provided. Don't worry. Your role as leader is not to provide answers for every question. You are a learner too. Read the question out loud (or write it on newsprint) and let the group respond. Encourage people to explain their answer to each question, even if the question is a simple true or false statement. If the group is silent, offer your own thoughts as a starting point. Reading each chapter before the group meets and thinking about each question beforehand will make the task a lot easier.

If you'd like, pass this book along from one leader to another. Each chapter is written separately to let your group proceed at it's own pace. While 40 minutes may be adequate for one group per chapter, others may want to take the whole hour. Still others may want to focus only on specific questions, so that they can cover two chapters in an hour. Try one chapter with the group and get a feel for how they would like to proceed.

Snapshot Summary. A one-sentence summary of both the current and previous chapters (chapter 1 summarizes the book as a whole) offers a quick review for participants and provides continuity throughout the study.

Relationship Questions. These questions are at the heart of the study and focus on our relationships with others, with God, and with the world. (The world encompasses the arenas of home, work, and church.) Faith is about relationships. Our faith reminds us of how God has acted in our lives through Jesus Christ, and how God continues to work in our lives today through the work of the Holy Spirit. These three areas of relationships—our relationship with others, with God, and with the world—can be answered as a whole or can be used to focus on a group's particular interest. For example, a prayer group might focus on the questions that deal with God; a social-action committee might want to focus on the world or on others. Or, a group might want to alternate using the various sections from week to week. These three sections of questions are also intended to provide closure for each session—people can focus on one section that interests them, rather than thinking they have to answer every question. Keep in mind, however, that all these areas are important aspects of our faith and often overlap as we live our faith out in the world.

Activities. You'll note that each chapter provides a group activity as well as an activity that can be done at home individually. These are "doing" activities rather than just "thinking" activities. If your group is hesitant or embarrassed to participate, start out slowly and offer lots of encouragement. These are nonthreatening exercises that may provide new learning experiences for many of the participants. Read each activity beforehand, in case you need materials such as paper, pencils, or crayons.

Prayer. The prayer can be read by the leader, by a volunteer, or by the group to close each session. It also can be read in advance by the leader to help prepare for each session.

However you or the group decide to proceed with this journey, keep an open mind that leaves room for the Spirit to work. Try to relax and enjoy the experience as you discover anew the insights and challenges of the Bible.

1. Yes, Lord, I Have Sinned, But I Have Several Excellent Excuses!

Snapshot Summary

Chapter 1 is a summary, noting ways we sin and the excuses we use to cover up those sins. We need to admit and acknowledge our sin to God, so that we might experience the rich and loving relationship God has for us.

Our Relationship with Others

1. "Our problem is not that we hesitate to *admit* anything; our problem is that we are learning how *to justify everything!*" (pp. 13-14). Do you agree or disagree?
2. Share a time when you were caught doing something you shouldn't have been doing. Did you offer any excuses? How did you feel?
3. In what ways do people excuse their sin?

Our Relationship with God

1. In which of the following ways do you excuse your sin to God—with words? With scapegoats? By blaming others? By blaming circumstances? By blaming evil spirits? Explain.
2. How do your excuses keep you away from God's love?
3. What helps you to accept God's forgiveness?

Our Relationship with the World

1. The excuse I hear most often at church is . . . .
2. In what ways do you, as a church or a group of believers, help others confess their sin and remind them of God's forgiveness and grace?
3. What is the best antidote for an excuse? Explain your answer.

Activities

As a group: Ask each person in the group to complete the following statement. Write down their responses on a large sheet of paper. "The best place or method for getting past excuses and getting into God's forgiveness and grace is . . ."

At home: Go to a place where you can have some privacy. Think of a past sin or deed for which you feel guilt or remorse. Think about, and write down if possible, the excuses you've given God for your behavior. Ask for God's forgiveness and thank God for the salvation you have received through Jesus Christ. Throw away your paper and read 1 John 1:5-10.

> **Prayer:** *Dear God, you see through all our excuses. Give us the courage to live in your love, forgiveness, and mercy. Amen.*

2. The Sin of Just Talking a Good Game

Snapshot Summary

Chapter 1 explored the various excuses we use to cover up our sins, even though God is ready and willing to forgive us. Chapter 2 challenges us to live out our lives of faith through word and deed, rather than through empty intentions.

Our Relationship with Others

1. Think of something important you said you were going to do, but didn't do in the end. What happened? What was the situation?
2. What word or deed done by another person had a positive impact on your life of faith?
3. Actions speak louder than words. True or false? Explain.

Our Relationship with God

1. How have you failed to follow through with God? What one thing can you do to get back on track?
2. Read the short poem at the bottom of page 28. How is God speaking to you through these words?
3. How could you begin to live out your faith through word or deed?

Our Relationship with the World

1. How can our faith become contagious for others?
2. How has your faith changed your life at home? At church? At work?
3. How can your church translate faith into action in your own community?

Activities

As a group: Ask each member to think about a "faith hero," a person who really lives out the faith from day to day. What stands out about this person? Have each member of the group, in turn, share his or her thoughts about this faith hero.

At home: Set aside time each day for the next week to pray. Make the time (5 to 60 minutes) and place (somewhere comfortable) consistent throughout the week. Write down your prayers in three areas: 1) Confession of sin; 2) Thanksgiving for God's forgiveness and salvation; and 3) Things you have learned about God. What did you discover in the process?

> *Prayer: Gracious God, we do know how to talk a good game. Turn our faith into action so that our beliefs and creeds can become deeds. Amen.*

3. The Sins That Reduce Us to Shameful Silence

Snapshot Summary

Chapter 2 challenged us to live our lives of faith through word and deed rather than through empty intentions. Here we see how ambition, jealousy, and hostility can hinder our relationship with God and with others.

Our Relationship with Others

1. Share a time with another person in the group when you were silent because of shame or doing something wrong.
2. In what ways can you be an ambitious servant for others?
3. Howt do you feel when you are praised by others?

Our Relationship with God

1. In what ways do you show "ruthless ambition," putting yourself before others or trying to appear better than others in your faith?
2. In what ways has jealously hindered your relationship with God?
3. "Whoever wants to be first must be last of all and servant of all" (Mark 9:35). What does this mean to you?

Our Relationship with the World

1. After thinking about the gossip that goes on at work, home, and church, complete the following statements. "I like gossip because . . . ." "The destructive thing about gossip is . . . ."
2. Have you ever felt that people in the church judged you because of how well you know the Bible? If so, how did this make you feel?
3. How can you praise others more at home, at work, or at church?

Activities

As a group: Jesus took a child in his arms to show the disciples that love is far more important than power or knowledge or influence, when it comes to doing God's will. On newsprint, write the three categories—POWER, KNOWLEDGE, LOVE. Ask the group to fill in ways our culture encourages the use of each of these. For example, you might write "academics" under KNOWLEDGE. After completing your list, circle those things that Jesus would encourage us to do.

At home: Read the story of Ruth from the Old Testament and consider what it means for your own life of faith.

> **Prayer:** *Dear Lord, like the disciples, we want to be praised and to feel important. Remind us that our true worth is found in you, rather than in things or other people. Amen.*

4. The Sin of Halfheartedness

Snapshot Summary

In chapter 3 we discovered how ruthless ambition, jealousy, and hostility can hinder our relationship with God. In this chapter we are challenged to commit our lives to God by letting God's love and Spirit win our battles for us.

Our Relationship with Others

1. From my experience, being generous to others (check all that apply): ____ always works; ____ only works with those who like me already; ____ is well worth the effort and risk; ____ just doesn't work in our society.
2. Share a time when you were tempted to retaliate. What were the circumstances? How did things turn out?
3. What does it mean for you to "turn the other cheek"?

Our Relationship with God

1. Check the following that apply and explain your answer:
   ____ I find it difficult to understand certain parts of the Bible.
   ____ I find faith difficult because I *do* understand the Bible.
2. Think of a time when you were painfully insulted by another person. Share with God why it hurt so much, then ask God to forgive that person.
3. Recall a time when God gave you the courage and power to turn the other cheek. How did you feel?

Our Relationship with the World

1. What "enemies" do you need to love at work? At church?
2. What "persecutors" should be part of your prayers?
3. How might your church, as a group, be asked to turn the other cheek?

Activities

As a group: Role-play a situation at work, home, or church, where "turning the other cheek" could be applied. Act out the situation twice, once when the cheek is turned and once when it is not. Discuss both situations and how people felt emotionally. Remember that groups may also need to turn a collective cheek.

At home: Write down the one thing that stood out for you most from chapter 4 and a way to implement this learning throughout the week.

> **Prayer:** Dear God, give me the courage to be fully committed to your love. Empower me with your Spirit to turn the other cheek. Amen.

5. The Sin of Spiritual Arrogance

Snapshot Summary

Chapter 4 challenged us to commit our lives to God's way by letting God's love and Spirit win our battles for us. This Chapter addresses the importance of helping others and how it can enrich our own lives of faith.

Our Relationship with Others

1. Were you ever helped by an unexpected source? How did you feel?
2. Have you ever helped someone unexpectedly? How did you feel?
3. For the most part, I think people (circle those that apply): want to help; are afraid to help; are not sure how to help.

Our Relationship with God

1. In what ways are you a first-class ticket holder with God—refusing to move or change amidst a troubled world?
2. Share a time when God came to your rescue. How did you feel?
3. One thing from my faith that gives me courage to act for others is . . . .

Our Relationship with the World

1. Do you relate to the church as though you had a first-class, second-class, or third-class ticket?
2. In what ways could your church make it easier for members to help others in the church or community?
3. Share a time when someone from the church ministered to you.

Activities

As a group: List the characteristics of third-class ticket-holders in your church. How do they get involved to solve problems? How might this study group be involved to help the church?

At home: It could be argued that as we are fed and loved by God, we are then able to serve and love others. Choose a different psalm to read every day for the next week. Begin with something familiar, such as Psalm 23. As you read, note: 1) how the psalmist speaks of God's power and activity in our lives; and 2) how you can use God's gifts to help others.

> **Prayer:** *Dear God, you work powerfully in our lives every day. Help us to discover this love and to share it with others. Amen.*

6. The Sins That Are Deceptive

Snapshot Summary

Chapter 5 discussed how helping others, being third-class ticket-holders, can enrich our own lives of faith. In this chapter we look at sins and attitudes that may not look like much, but in their own way, keep us from God.

Our Relationship with Others

1. In 10 words or less, define sin.
2. Do you think we pay more attention to the "scarlet," or obvious sins, than we do to the "gray" sins? Why or why not?
3. Which sin do you think is most hurtful to God? To others?
4. Explain why you agree or disagree with the following: "Being polite is the same as being appreciative or thankful."

Our Relationship with God

1. The best advice I received about keeping my inner life clean was . . . .
2. What are the "gray" sins you encounter most in your relationship with God?
3. In what ways can you show your appreciation to God?
4. What helps you to make God the center of your life?

Our Relationship with the World

1. For which things in your life are you most grateful? For which of these things have you thanked God through praise or prayer?
2. How do you show your appreciation to God in your worship service?
3. The "one big Sin, which prompts and produces all the others, is the worship of self rather than of God" (p. 57). In what ways do you agree or disagree with this statement?

Activities

As a group: Hand out paper and crayons to the group. Ask each person to write a poem or draw a picture of something for which they are particularly grateful.

At home: It is a Jewish custom to thank God 100 times a day. For example, "Thank you, God, for the rain. Thank you for the sun. Thank you for people who care for me." Over the next week, write down 100 things for which you can thank God.

> **Prayer:** *Thank you for all you've given us, God. Help our lives to be prayers of thankfulness. Amen.*

7. The Sin of Overreaction

Snapshot Summary

In chapter 6 we looked at deceptive sins and attitudes that can separate us from God. Chapter 7 explores how overreaction to situations at home, in the church, and with God can make bad situations even worse.

Our Relationship with Others

1. Describe a time when you overreacted to a situation.
2. Share a maxim or saying that comes to mind when you think of making hasty decisions.
3. When did being patient really pay off for you?
4. What has helped you to be more patient in your life of faith?

Our Relationship with God

1. Share a time when, in your haste, you reacted to a situation rather than waiting for God's response.
2. From your own experience, what is the hardest thing about waiting for God's response?
3. It has been said that God's answers to prayer are: *yes, no,* and *wait awhile.* Do you find this helpful in waiting for God's response to prayer? Why or why not?

Our Relationship with the World

1. Think of a time you overreacted as a church. What was the situation? How was the situation resolved?
2. Check all that apply. Hasty decisions are best corrected by:____ forgiveness; ____ understanding; ____ ignoring the problem; ____ prayer; ____ other _____.
3. Write down three ways you can be more patient in your responses at work, at home, and in your faith life.

Activities

As a group: Brainstorm ways your church can be more patient in its ministry to others.
At home: Write a poem, or word play, or draw a picture using the letters p-a-t-i-e-n-c-e. Use them in combination, as a pattern, or list each letter vertically down the page as an acrostic puzzle. (An acrostic might begin: Prayer At Times Is Easy . . . .)

Prayer: *Dear God, forgive us for the times we have overreacted. Help us to be patient and to trust in your power, guidance, and timing. Amen.*

8. The Sin of Hostility

Snapshot Summary

Chapter 7 explored how overreaction to situations at home, in the church, and with God can make bad situations even worse. This chapter uncovers ways to bring peace into our lives through forgiveness, love, thoughtfulness, and by speaking up for others.

Our Relationship with Others

1. Think of three walls in the world that keep others out.
2. Think of three walls in the world that keep us fenced out.
3. The most troublesome thing in the Bible to me is . . . .
4. What image comes to mind when you think of the word *forgiveness*? Share this image with another person.

Our Relationship with God

1. What walls have you built up to keep God away?
2. God forgives all my sins. True or False? Explain your answer.
3. What bridges have you discovered that keep you in contact with God?

Our Relationship with the World

1. In what ways has your church built up walls? Think of programs, policies, building limitations (e.g., no access for the physically challenged), and so on that can keep people away.
2. Share a wall your church has removed, or a time when the church removed a wall for you.
3. Share your favorite saying about love.

Activities

As a group: Have the group bring in some old magazines. Ask the group to make a collage of the walls we build up around us in the world and in our community. When the collage is finished, discuss ways to remove each of these walls, or ways you can speak up for those hurt by these walls.
At home: Mark the statement below that challenges you most.
_____ it's O.K. to forgive; _____ it's O.K. to love all people; _____ it's O.K. to think; _____ it's O.K. to speak out for others.
Find two ways in the upcoming week to live out this challenge in your life of faith.

> **Prayer:** *Dear Lord, make us instruments of your peace. Guide us with your Spirit to build bridges in our homes and communities. Amen.*

9. The Sin of Presumptuousness

Snapshot Summary

Chapter 8 looked at forgiveness, love, thoughtfulness, and speaking up for others as ways to bring peace into our hostile worlds. Chapter 9 examines what it means to take God and others for granted.

Our Relationship with Others

1. Look up the word *presumptuous* in a dictionary. What, if anything, surprised you about its meaning?
2. Think of a time in childhood when you really felt important. Also think of a similar time in adulthood. How are the two events similar? How are they different? Share your memories and insights.
3. Choose one of the responses below and explain your choice.
   (a) we know all there is to know about God; (b) we know quite a bit about God; (c) we know very little about God.

Our Relationship with God

1. Check the statement below with which you agree most.
   _____ I am an important person to God; _____ I am not an important person to God; _____ I am occasionally an important person to God.
2. How have you limited, or underestimated, God's power in your life?
3. Share a time when God surprised you.

Our Relationship with the World

1. In what ways did your family make you feel important as a child?
2. Write down in 10 words or less what it means to feel important.
3. "Good, healthy faith is humble faith that keeps on growing. It is not content with one experience with God, or a few simplistic religious notions" (p. 80). Share an example of this kind of "healthy faith."

Activities

As a group: Have a 12" x 24" sheet of foil available for each person. Ask each person to shape it, crumple it, tear it, or draw on it to represent a time when she or he felt particularly important to God. Ask volunteers to share their works of art and stories.

At home: Think of someone special to you. Find one nonverbal way and one verbal way to tell that person of your love.

Prayer: *Gracious God, I am so important to you that you sent your Son to die for me. Thank you. Amen.*

10. The Sin of Losing Our Spiritual Balance

Snapshot Summary

Chapter 9 looked at what it means to take God and others for granted. Chapter 10 examines what it means to keep our lives balanced through a sense of priorities, a sense of humor, a sense of the holy habits, and a sense of partnership with God.

Our Relationship with Others

1. Which is more common in our society, *rescue* medicine or *preventive* medicine (p. 89)?
2. Do you think a sense of humor is important? Why or why not?
3. In groups of two or three, choose an example from the Bible that shows Jesus' sense of humor.

Our Relationship with God

1. One thing that makes me feel chained up in my life of faith is . . . .
2. What inspires you, or gives you courage, to keep God a priority in your life?
3. Which of the following "spiritual vitamins" (p. 91) do you find most invigorating: church attendance; prayer; studying Scripture; helping others; striving daily to live the faith?

Our Relationship with the World

1. The most important thing in my life is . . . .
2. Who was the comedian, or funny person, in your family?
3. In what ways can your church be a co-worker with God in the community? In the world? On Sundays?

Activities

As a group: Debate the following statement in two groups: "The devil made me do it."
At home: Choose one stanza of the hymn on page 93. Meditate on it daily, letting it fill you with God's hope and power.

Prayer: *Breathe on me, Spirit of God. Breathe on me, Son of God. Breathe on me, Creator God. Fill me with life. Amen.*

11. Sin . . . and Redemption

Snapshot Summary

Chapter 10 covered ways to keep our lives balanced. This chapter challenges us to let God work in our lives so that we might be changed into people of God.

Our Relationship with Others

1. Do you think it is easy for people to change? Why or why not?
2. Choose one of the following and explain your answer. God is at work in our lives: all of the time; some of the time; very little of the time.
3. *Redemption* "means that bad things can be changed to good things, bad habits can be replaced with good habits, defeats can be turned into victories, weak people can be converted into strong, courageous people" (p. 95). Share an example of redemption from your own life.

Our Relationship with God

1. What in your life needs to be changed or converted?
2. Choose all those that apply. Discuss your choices. God can change me: through the Holy Spirit; only if I want to be changed; through other people.
3. Think of a time God brought about positive change in your life. Share this occasion, if you'd like, with another person. Pray, thanking God for the work of the Spirit to bring about change in our lives.

Our Relationship with the World

1. Think of something at work or at home that needs to be changed. How might God use you to help change things positively?
2. What events in the world need to be redeemed or changed? What can you do as an individual to help with this change?
3. In what ways is God working through your church to change the community? To change your congregation?

Activities

As a group: Watch a video or a segment of a TV show. How were the characters changed or converted? Were changes positive? Negative? Explain.
At home: Read the story of Joseph from the Old Testament in Genesis 37:1–50:26. Notice how God worked good in the midst of evil.

> **Prayer:** *Holy Lord, move your Spirit within us to change us, so that we might do your will in loving those around us. Amen.*

12. Sin . . . and Grace

Snapshot Summary

Chapter 11 explored ways in which God redeemed—or changed—people, words, things, and events. Chapter 12 discusses ways we get lost in sin and how God finds and saves us through grace.

Our Relationship with Others

1. Think of a time you were lost. Share this experience with one or two other people.
2. Share a time you remember being found or finding something you had lost. How did you feel?
3. What, to you, is the source of happiness in life?

Our Relationship with God

1. Check all the following that apply. God finds me:
   _____ when I go to church.
   _____ when I read the Bible.
   _____ in prayer.
   _____ in the midst of others that care for me.
   _____ other. _____
2. One way to keep my relationship with God fresh and vibrant and alive is . . . .
3. What is your favorite place to share time with God?
4. When is God closest to you during the worship service?
5. In what ways have you experienced God's grace?

Our Relationship with the World

1. Recall a time when your family lost and then found something valuable.
2. Think of a relative, or a person at work or at church who seems lost. What can you do to help him or her find the way back home?
3. What person influenced you most in your walk of faith as a child? As a teenager? As an adult? How did he or she impact your faith?

Activities

As a group: "Faith is friendship with God!" (p. 104). Make two equal columns on a sheet of newsprint. Title one column "Friendship with others." Title the other column "Friendship with God." Brainstorm ways people can keep their friendships alive in each category. How are the columns similar? How are they different?

At home: Write a letter of encouragement and support to someone you know is lost. Pray that God will work powerfully in this person's life so that they might experience God's love and forgiveness.

Prayer: *Great Shepherd, you seek us out daily to love us and save us. Ever remind us that you will never leave us or forsake us. Amen.*